THE AUSTRALIAN
Women's Weekly
little pies&cakes

acp
books

CONTENTS

SAVOURY

BEEF AND ONION PARTY PIES

1 tablespoon vegetable oil
1 medium brown onion (150g), chopped finely
450g beef mince
2 tablespoons tomato paste
2 tablespoons worcestershire sauce
2 tablespoons powdered gravy mix
¾ cup (180ml) water
3 sheets ready-rolled shortcrust pastry
1 egg, beaten lightly
2 sheets ready-rolled puff pastry

1 Heat oil in large frying pan; cook onion, stirring, until
onion softens. Add beef; cook, stirring, until beef changes
colour. Add paste, sauce, and blended gravy powder and
the water; bring to the boil, stirring. Reduce heat; simmer,
uncovered, about 10 minutes or until thickened slightly; cool.
2 Preheat oven to 200°C/180°C fan-forced. Grease two
12-hole (2-tablespoons/40ml) deep flat-based patty pans.
3 Cut twenty-four 7cm rounds from shortcrust pastry; press
into pan holes. Divide beef mixture among pastry cases.
Brush edges with a little of the egg.
4 Cut twenty-four 6cm rounds from puff pastry; top pies
with puff pastry lids. Press edges firmly to seal; brush lids
with remaining egg. Cut a small slit in top of each pie.
5 Bake about 20 minutes or until browned lightly. Stand
pies in pan 5 minutes before serving.
preparation time *25 minutes*
cooking time *35 minutes* makes 24
nutritional count per pie *11.2g total fat*
(5.4g saturated fat); 790kJ (189 cal);
15.5g carbohydrate; 6.4g protein; 0.7g fibre

TOMATO, FETTA AND PANCETTA FRITTATA

6 slices (100g) pancetta, chopped coarsely
100g fetta cheese, crumbled
¼ cup (20g) finely grated parmesan cheese
⅓ cup coarsely chopped fresh basil
6 eggs
⅔ cup (160ml) cream
9 mini roma tomatoes (150g), halved lengthways

1 Preheat oven to 180°C/160°C fan-forced. Grease six-hole (¾-cup/180ml) texas muffin pan; line bases with baking paper.
2 Layer pancetta, cheeses and basil in pan holes. Whisk eggs and cream in medium bowl; pour into pan holes. Top each frittata with three tomato halves.
3 Bake about 25 minutes. Stand in pan 5 minutes before turning out.

preparation time *10 minutes*
cooking time *25 minutes* makes *6*
nutritional count per frittata *24.1g total fat (13.3g saturated fat); 1170kJ (280 cal); 1.6g carbohydrate; 14.9g protein; 0.4g fibre*

chicken and mushroom party pies

moroccan lamb party pies

CHICKEN AND MUSHROOM PARTY PIES

1 tablespoon olive oil
1 small brown onion (80g) chopped finely
1 clove garlic, crushed
400g chicken mince
100g mushrooms, chopped finely
2 teaspoons plain flour
¾ cup (180ml) cream
2 tablespoons finely chopped fresh chives
3 sheets ready-rolled shortcrust pastry
1 egg, beaten lightly
2 sheets ready-rolled puff pastry
2 teaspoons sesame seeds

1 Heat oil in medium frying pan; cook onion and garlic, stirring, until onion softens. Add chicken and mushrooms; cook, stirring, until chicken changes colour. Add flour; cook, stirring, 1 minute. Gradually stir in cream; cook, stirring, until mixture boils and thickens. Stir in chives; cool.
2 Preheat oven to 200°C/180°C fan-forced. Grease two 12-hole (2-tablespoons/40ml) deep flat-based patty pans.
3 Cut twenty-four 7cm rounds from shortcrust pastry; press into pan holes. Brush edges with a little of the egg. Spoon chicken mixture into pastry cases.
4 Cut twenty-four 6cm rounds from puff pastry; top pies with puff pastry lids. Press edges firmly to seal; brush lids with remaining egg, sprinkle with sesame seeds. Cut a small slit in top of each pie.
5 Bake about 20 minutes or until browned lightly. Stand pies in pan 5 minutes before serving.

preparation time *25 minutes*
cooking time *30 minutes* makes *24*
nutritional count per pie *14.5g total fat
(7.4g saturated fat); 895kJ (214 cal);
14.8g carbohydrate; 6g protein; 0.8g fibre*

tip We used chicken breast mince for this recipe.

MOROCCAN LAMB PARTY PIES

1 tablespoon vegetable oil
1 small brown onion (80g), chopped finely
1 clove garlic, crushed
400g lamb mince
2 teaspoons ground cumin
1 cup (280g) undrained canned crushed tomatoes
¼ cup (40g) roasted pine nuts
2 tablespoons finely chopped raisins
2 tablespoons finely chopped fresh coriander
3 sheets ready-rolled shortcrust pastry
1 egg, beaten lightly
2 sheets ready-rolled puff pastry

1 Heat oil in medium frying pan; cook onion and garlic, stirring, until onion softens. Add lamb; cook, stirring, until lamb changes colour. Add cumin; cook, stirring, until fragrant. Add tomatoes; bring to the boil. Reduce heat; simmer, uncovered, about 5 minutes or until thickened slightly. Stir in nuts, raisins and coriander; cool.
2 Preheat oven to 200°C/180°C fan-forced. Grease two 12-hole (2-tablespoons/40ml) deep flat-based patty pans.
3 Cut twenty-four 7cm rounds from shortcrust pastry; press into pan holes. Brush edges with a little of the egg. Spoon lamb mixture into pastry cases.
4 Cut twenty-four 6cm rounds from puff pastry; top pies with puff pastry lids. Press edges firmly to seal; brush lids with egg. Cut a small slit in top of each pie.
5 Bake about 20 minutes or until browned lightly. Stand pies in pan 5 minutes before serving.

serving idea Accompany with mango chutney.
preparation time *25 minutes*
cooking time *35 minutes* makes *24*
nutritional count per pie *12.2g total fat
(5.5g saturated fat); 828kJ (198 cal);
15.6g carbohydrate; 6.2g protein; 0.9g fibre*

POTATO AND ANCHOVY GRATIN

700g potatoes
1 small brown onion (80g)
12 undrained anchovy fillets in oil
300ml cream
½ cup (125ml) milk
½ teaspoon freshly ground black pepper
2 tablespoons finely chopped fresh dill

1 Preheat oven to 200°C/180°C fan-forced. Grease six-hole (¾-cup/180ml) texas muffin pan; line each hole with two criss-crossed 5cm x 20cm strips of baking paper.
2 Using sharp knife, mandoline or V-slicer, cut potatoes and onion into very thin slices.
3 Drain and reserve oil from anchovies (you need 2 teaspoons oil); chop anchovies coarsely. Layer potato, onion and anchovy in pan holes, starting and finishing with potato.
4 Heat reserved anchovy oil, cream, milk and pepper in small saucepan; pour over potato mixture. Bake, in oven, about 35 minutes or until potato is tender. Stand in pan 10 minutes. Using baking-paper strips as lifters, gently remove gratin from pan holes.
5 Serve gratin sprinkled with dill.
preparation time *15 minutes*
cooking time *40 minutes* makes *6*
nutritional count per gratin *22.9g total fat (14.9g saturated fat); 1241kJ (297 cal); 16.1g carbohydrate; 6.3g protein; 1.8g fibre*

tip We used medium-sized potatoes for this recipe.

HUEVOS RANCHEROS

6 x 15cm corn tortillas
125g can kidney beans, rinsed, drained
½ cup (130g) bottled chunky tomato salsa
1 small tomato (90g), chopped coarsely
2 tablespoons coarsely chopped fresh coriander
6 eggs
½ cup (60g) coarsely grated cheddar cheese
1 small avocado (200g), chopped coarsely
1 tablespoon lime juice

1 Preheat oven to 200°C/180°C fan-forced. Grease six-hole (¾-cup/180ml) texas muffin pan.
2 Soften tortillas according to manufacturer's instructions. Gently press one tortilla into each pan hole to form a cup.
3 Combine beans, salsa, tomato and coriander in small bowl; divide half the bean mixture among tortilla cups. Break one egg into each cup. Sprinkle with cheese.
4 Bake about 12 minutes or until eggs are cooked.
5 Meanwhile, stir avocado and juice into remaining bean mixture.
6 Serve huevos rancheros topped with avocado mixture.
serving ideas Sour cream and lime wedges.
preparation time *15 minutes*
cooking time *12 minutes* makes *6*
nutritional count per huevos rancheros *14.5g total fat (5g saturated fat); 961kJ (230 cal); 11.8g carbohydrate; 12.1g protein; 2.8g fibre*

potato and anchovy gratin

huevos rancheros

parmesan, chilli and herb baked ricotta

pizza muffins

PARMESAN, CHILLI AND HERB BAKED RICOTTA

½ cup finely chopped mixed fresh herbs
2 fresh long red chillies, chopped finely
1 teaspoon sea salt flakes
½ cup (40g) finely grated parmesan cheese
3⅓ cups (800g) ricotta cheese
2 eggs
1 teaspoon finely grated lemon rind

1 Preheat oven to 120°C/100°C fan-forced. Grease six-hole (¾-cup/180ml) texas muffin pan; line bases with baking paper.
2 Combine herbs, chilli and salt in small bowl; spread evenly onto oven tray. Roast about 20 minutes or until dried; cool.
3 Stir parmesan into herb mixture. Place 1 tablespoon of herb mixture into each pan hole; shake pan to coat bases and sides of holes with mixture.
4 Increase temperature to 180°C/160°C fan-forced.
5 Combine ricotta, eggs, rind and remaining herb mixture in medium bowl. Divide mixture among pan holes; smooth surface with a spatula, pressing down firmly to remove any air bubbles.
6 Bake ricotta about 20 minutes or until firm. Stand in pan 15 minutes. Use palette knife to loosen ricotta from side of pan before turning out, top-side down. Cool.
serving idea Accompany with lavash crisps.
preparation time *15 minutes*
(plus standing and cooling time)
cooking time *45 minutes* makes *6*
nutritional count per baked ricotta *19g total fat (11.5g saturated fat); 1053kJ (252 cal); 1.7g carbohydrate; 18.9g protein; 0.3g fibre*

tip We used basil, flat-leaf parsley and oregano for the herbs in this recipe.

PIZZA MUFFINS

4 rindless bacon rashers (260g), chopped finely
4 green onions, chopped finely
3 slices (120g) bottled roasted red capsicum, chopped finely
¾ cup (75g) pizza cheese
½ teaspoon dried chilli flakes

basic muffin mix
2 cups (300g) self-raising flour
80g butter, melted
1 egg
1 cup (250ml) buttermilk

1 Preheat oven to 200°C/180°C fan-forced. Grease 12-hole (⅓-cup/80ml) muffin pan.
2 Cook bacon in heated medium frying pan, stirring, until browned lightly. Add onion; cook, stirring, until onion softens. Cool.
3 Meanwhile make basic muffin mix.
4 Add capsicum, cheese, chilli and bacon mixture to basic muffin mix; mix gently to combine. Do not over-mix; mixture should be lumpy.
5 Divide mixture among holes. Bake, in oven, about 20 minutes. Stand muffins 5 minutes before turning, top-side up, onto wire rack. Serve muffins warm
basic muffin mix Sift flour into medium bowl; stir in combined butter, egg and buttermilk.
serving idea Accompany warm muffins with butter.
preparation time *20 minutes*
cooking time *25 minutes* makes *12*
nutritional count per muffin *11.8g total fat (6.1g saturated fat); 928kJ (222 cal); 17g carbohydrate; 10.7g protein; 2.9g fibre*

BEEF PIES WITH POLENTA TOPS

500g beef chuck steak, cut into 4cm pieces
1 tablespoon plain flour
2 tablespoons olive oil
1 small brown onion (80g), chopped finely
2 cloves garlic, crushed
100g button mushrooms, halved
½ cup (125ml) dry red wine
½ cup (125ml) beef stock
1 cup (280g) canned crushed tomatoes
1 small red capsicum (150g), chopped coarsely
¼ cup (40g) seeded black olives
¼ cup (35g) coarsely chopped, drained
    sun-dried tomatoes in oil
⅓ cup coarsely chopped fresh basil
2 sheets ready-rolled shortcrust pastry
1 large potato (300g), chopped coarsely
20g butter
1 tablespoon milk
¼ cup (20g) finely grated parmesan cheese

soft polenta
¼ cup (60ml) chicken stock
¾ cup (180ml) milk
¼ cup (40g) polenta
¼ cup (20g) finely grated parmesan cheese

1 Coat beef in flour; shake off excess. Heat half the oil in large saucepan; cook beef, in batches, until browned.
2 Heat remaining oil in same pan; cook onion, garlic and mushrooms, stirring, until vegetables soften. Add wine; bring to the boil. Return beef to pan with stock and crushed tomatoes; bring to the boil. Reduce heat; simmer, covered, 1 hour. Uncover, stir in capsicum, olives and sun-dried tomato; simmer 15 minutes or until sauce thickens; cool. Stir in basil.
3 Preheat oven to 180°C/160°C fan-forced. Grease six-hole (¾-cup/180ml) texas muffin pan.
4 Make soft polenta.
5 Meanwhile, boil, steam or microwave potato until tender; drain. Mash potato with butter and milk in medium bowl until smooth.
6 Gently swirl hot polenta mixture into hot potato mixture.
7 Cut six 12cm rounds from shortcrust pastry; press into pan holes. Divide beef mixture among pastry cases; top with potato and polenta mixture, sprinkle with cheese.
8 Bake, in oven, about 30 minutes. Stand pies in pan 5 minutes before using a palette knife to loosen pie from side of tin and ease out.

soft polenta Combine stock and milk in small saucepan; bring to the boil. Gradually stir polenta into stock mixture. Reduce heat; cook, stirring, about 5 minutes or until polenta thickens. Stir in cheese.

preparation time *35 minutes*
cooking time *2 hours* makes *6*
nutritional count per pie *32.3g total fat*
(14.6g saturated fat); 2533kJ (606 cal);
44.8g carbohydrate; 28.6g protein; 4.5g fibre

spanish tortilla

roasted capsicum and goats cheese terrine

SPANISH TORTILLA

500g potatoes, sliced thinly
1 tablespoon olive oil
1 medium brown onion (150g), sliced thinly
1 chorizo sausage (170g), sliced thinly
4 green onions, chopped coarsely
5 eggs
1 cup (250ml) cream
1 clove garlic, crushed
¾ cup (90g) coarsely grated cheddar cheese

1 Preheat oven to 180°C/160°C fan-forced. Grease six-hole (¾-cup/180ml) texas muffin pan; line bases with baking paper.
2 Boil, steam or microwave potato until tender; drain.
3 Meanwhile, heat oil in medium frying pan; cook brown onion, stirring, until onion softens. Add chorizo; cook, stirring, until chorizo crisps. Stir in green onion; drain mixture on absorbent paper.
4 Whisk eggs in medium bowl with cream and garlic. Divide potato, chorizo mixture and cheese among pan holes. Pour egg mixture into pan holes.
5 Bake, in oven, about 30 minutes or until set. Stand tortillas in pan 5 minutes before turning out, top-side up.
serving idea Serve tortillas with a spinach salad.
preparation time *15 minutes*
cooking time *40 minutes* makes *6*
nutritional count per tortilla *39.1g total fat (20g saturated fat); 2019kJ (483 cal); 14.7g carbohydrate; 18.1g protein; 2.3g fibre*

ROASTED CAPSICUM AND GOATS CHEESE TERRINE

3 large red capsicums (1kg)
1½ cups (360g) ricotta cheese, chopped coarsely
250g firm goats cheese, chopped coarsely
¼ cup finely chopped fresh chives
2 tablespoons lemon juice
1 clove garlic, crushed

spinach and walnut pesto
¼ cup (20g) finely grated parmesan cheese
100g baby spinach leaves
¼ cup (25g) roasted walnuts
1 clove garlic, quartered
¼ cup (60ml) olive oil
2 tablespoons lemon juice
1 tablespoon water

1 Preheat oven to 240°C/220°C fan-forced. Grease six holes of eight-hole (½-cup/125ml) petite loaf pan. Line base and two long sides of each hole with a strip of baking paper, extending 5cm over sides.
2 Halve capsicums; discard seeds and membranes. Place on oven tray; roast, skin-side up, about 15 minutes or until skin blisters and blackens. Cover with plastic wrap for 5 minutes then peel away skin. Cut capsicum into strips; line base and two long sides of pan holes with capsicum strips, extending 2cm over edges.
3 Combine remaining ingredients in medium bowl; spoon cheese mixture into pan holes, pressing down firmly. Fold capsicum strips over to enclose filling. Cover; refrigerate 1 hour.
4 Meanwhile, make spinach and walnut pesto.
5 Carefully remove terrines from pan holes; serve with spinach and walnut pesto; sprinkle with chopped fresh chives.
spinach and walnut pesto Process cheese, spinach, nuts and garlic until chopped finely. With motor operating, gradually add combined oil, juice and the water in a thin, steady stream; process until pesto is smooth.
preparation time *30 minutes (plus refrigeration time)*
cooking time *15 minutes* makes *6*
nutritional count per terrine *26.8g total fat (10.8g saturated fat); 1417kJ (339 cal); 7.5g carbohydrate; 16.5g protein; 2.6g fibre*

SMOKED OCEAN TROUT AND ASPARAGUS FRITTATA WITH ROCKET PESTO

18 asparagus spears (340g), trimmed
150g sliced smoked ocean trout, chopped coarsely
¼ cup (20g) finely grated parmesan cheese
6 eggs
⅔ cup (160ml) cream

rocket pesto
1½ cups baby rocket leaves
2 tablespoons roasted pine nuts
1 clove garlic, chopped coarsely
2 tablespoons finely grated parmesan cheese
¼ cup (60ml) olive oil
1 tablespoon lemon juice

1 Preheat oven to 180°C/160°C fan-forced. Grease six-hole (¾-cup/180ml) texas muffin pan; line bases with baking paper.
2 Cut asparagus into 4cm lengths; reserve asparagus tips. Layer remaining asparagus, trout and cheese in pan holes. Whisk eggs and cream in medium bowl; pour into pan holes. Top each frittata with three asparagus tips.
3 Bake about 25 minutes. Stand in pan 5 minutes; using palette knife, loosen frittata from edge of pan before turning out, top-side up.
4 Meanwhile, make rocket pesto.
5 Serve frittata, top-side up, with rocket pesto.
rocket pesto Blend or process rocket, nuts, garlic and cheese until finely chopped. With motor operating, gradually add combined oil and juice in a thin, steady stream; process until pesto is smooth.
preparation time *15 minutes*
cooking time *25 minutes* makes 6
nutritional count per frittata *32.5g total fat (12.2g saturated fat); 1542kJ (369 cal); 2.1g carbohydrate; 17.6g protein; 1.1g fibre*

ROAST KUMARA AND SPINACH FRITTATA

2 medium kumara (800g)
1 tablespoon olive oil
2 teaspoons ground cumin
50g baby spinach leaves, chopped coarsely
¼ cup (20g) finely grated parmesan cheese
6 eggs, beaten lightly
⅔ cup (160ml) cream

1 Preheat oven to 180°C/160°C fan-forced. Grease six-hole (¾-cup/180ml) texas muffin pan; line bases with baking paper.
2 Peel kumara; cut into 5mm slices. Combine kumara, oil and cumin in large, shallow baking dish; roast about 20 minutes or until tender. Cool 10 minutes.
3 Divide spinach, cheese then kumara among pan holes, finishing with kumara.
4 Whisk egg and cream in medium bowl; pour into pan holes.
5 Bake about 25 minutes. Stand in pan 5 minutes; using palette knife, loosen frittata from edge of pan before turning out, top-side up.
preparation time *15 minutes*
cooking time *45 minutes* makes 6
nutritional count per frittata *21g total fat (10.3g saturated fat); 1267kJ (303 cal); 16.9g carbohydrate; 10.8g protein; 2.3g fibre*

smoked ocean trout and asparagus frittata with rocket pesto

roast kumara and spinach frittata

YORKSHIRE PUDDINGS WITH BEEF AND RED WINE STEW

800g beef chuck steak, cut into 4cm pieces
2 tablespoons plain flour
⅓ cup (80ml) olive oil
40g butter
6 shallots (150g), halved
2 cloves garlic, crushed
150g button mushrooms, halved
1 large carrot (180g), chopped coarsely
1 cup (250ml) dry red wine
2 tablespoons tomato paste
1 cup (250ml) beef stock
2 tablespoons worcestershire sauce
2 sprigs fresh thyme
¼ cup coarsely chopped fresh chives

yorkshire pudding batter
⅓ cup (50g) plain flour
¼ teaspoon salt
⅓ cup (80ml) milk
1 egg

1 Coat beef in flour; shake off excess. Heat 2 tablespoons of the oil in large saucepan; cook beef, in batches, until browned all over.
2 Melt half the butter in same pan; cook shallot, garlic, mushrooms and carrot, stirring, until vegetables soften. Add wine; bring to the boil. Return beef to pan with paste, stock, sauce and thyme; bring to the boil. Reduce heat; simmer, covered, 1¼ hours. Uncover; simmer about 15 minutes or until sauce thickens. Stir in chives.
3 Meanwhile, make yorkshire pudding batter.
4 Preheat oven to 240°C/220°C fan-forced. Melt remaining butter; divide combined melted butter and remaining oil among four holes of six-hole (¾-cup/180ml) texas muffin pan. Heat pan in oven 3 minutes. Remove pan from oven; immediately divide batter among hot pan holes.
5 Return pan to oven; bake about 12 minutes or until puddings are well browned. Serve puddings, top-side up, with stew; sprinkle with chopped fresh chives.

yorkshire pudding batter Sift flour and salt into small bowl. Whisk in combined milk and egg until smooth. Pour into jug, cover; stand 20 minutes.

preparation time *25 minutes*
cooking time *1 hour 50 minutes* serves *4*
nutritional count per serving *38.2g total fat (12.8g saturated fat); 2788kJ (667 cal); 21.1g carbohydrate; 48.4g protein; 4.1g fibre*

OLIVE AND TOMATO BAKED RICOTTA

¾ cup (60g) finely grated parmesan cheese
3⅓ cups (800g) ricotta cheese
2 eggs
1 clove garlic, crushed
1 teaspoon finely grated lemon rind
⅔ cup (100g) drained semi-dried tomatoes in oil,
   chopped finely
⅔ cup (100g) seeded black olives, chopped finely
¼ cup fresh basil leaves, chopped finely

1 Preheat oven to 180°C/160°C fan-forced. Grease
six-hole (¾-cup/180ml) texas muffin pan; line bases with
baking paper.
2 Divide half the parmesan among pan holes; shake pan
to coat bases and sides with cheese.
3 Combine ricotta, eggs, garlic, rind, tomato, olive, basil
and remaining parmesan in medium bowl. Divide mixture
among pan holes; smooth surface with spatula, pressing
down firmly to remove any air bubbles.
4 Bake about 20 minutes or until firm. Stand in pan
15 minutes before turning out, top-side down; cool.
serving ideas Drizzle with olive oil then sprinkle with fresh
basil leaves; serve with a flat bread of your choice.
preparation time *15 minutes*
cooking time *20 minutes* makes 6
nutritional count per baked ricotta *21.6g total fat
(12.4g saturated fat); 1379kJ (330 cal);
11.2g carbohydrate; 22g protein; 2.7g fibre*

DUKKAH-CRUSTED BAKED RICOTTA

3⅓ cups (800g) ricotta cheese
2 eggs
¼ cup (50g) finely chopped preserved lemon
2 tablespoons roasted hazelnuts
2 tablespoons unsalted roasted pistachios
1 tablespoon ground coriander
1 tablespoon ground cumin
2 teaspoons sumac
2 tablespoons sesame seeds, roasted

1 Preheat oven to 180°C/160°C fan-forced. Grease
six-hole (¾-cup/180ml) texas muffin pan; line bases with
baking paper.
2 Combine ricotta, eggs and lemon in medium bowl.
Divide mixture among pan holes; smooth surface with
spatula, pressing down firmly to remove any air bubbles.
3 Bake ricotta about 20 minutes or until firm. Stand in
pan 15 minutes before turning out, top-side down.
4 Meanwhile, to make dukkah, dry-fry nuts in small frying
pan over medium heat until browned lightly. Add spices;
cook, stirring, about 1 minute or until fragrant. Process
mixture until fine; stir in seeds.
5 Place dukkah on tray; gently roll warm baked ricotta in
dukkah to coat; cool. Serve ricotta, top-side down, with
remaining dukkah.
serving ideas Drizzle with olive oil, and serve with thick
slices of warm toast.
preparation time *15 minutes*
cooking time *20 minutes* makes 6
nutritional count per baked ricotta *23.4g total fat
(10.7g saturated fat); 1237kJ (296 cal);
2.8g carbohydrate; 18.5g protein; 1.4g fibre*

olive and tomato baked ricotta

dukkah-crusted baked ricotta

moussaka timbales

baked cheesy polenta with salsa

MOUSSAKA TIMBALES

¼ cup (60ml) olive oil
1 medium brown onion (150g), chopped finely
2 cloves garlic, crushed
500g lamb mince
400g can diced tomatoes
1 tablespoon tomato paste
½ cup (125ml) dry white wine
1 teaspoon ground cinnamon
¼ teaspoon ground nutmeg
¼ cup coarsely chopped fresh flat-leaf parsley
¼ cup (40g) roasted pine nuts
2 small eggplants (460g)

1 Heat 1 tablespoon of the oil in large frying pan; cook onion and garlic, stirring, until onion softens. Add lamb; cook, stirring, until lamb changes colour. Stir in undrained tomatoes, paste, wine and spices; bring to the boil. Reduce heat; simmer, uncovered, about 20 minutes or until liquid has evaporated. Cool; stir in parsley and nuts.
2 Meanwhile, slice eggplant lengthways into 3mm thin slices using sharp knife, mandolin or V-slicer. Mix eggplant slices with remaining oil; cook on heated grill plate until browned lightly. Cool.
3 Preheat oven to 180°C/160°C fan-forced. Grease six-hole (¾-cup/180ml) texas muffin pan. Line each pan hole with eggplant slices, overlapping slightly and extending 4cm above edge of hole. Divide lamb mixture among eggplant cases. Fold eggplant over to enclose filling.
4 Bake about 10 minutes. Stand in pan 5 minutes before serving, top-side down. Sprinkle with chopped fresh flat-leaf parsley.

serving idea Accompany with tzatziki, a Greek dip made from yogurt, diced cucumber and garlic.
preparation time *25 minutes*
cooking time *50 minutes* makes 6
nutritional count per timbale *19.9g total fat (4g saturated fat); 1262kJ (302 cal); 6.3g carbohydrate; 19.8g protein; 3.7g fibre*

BAKED CHEESY POLENTA WITH SALSA

2 cups (500ml) chicken stock
2 cups (500ml) water
1 cup (170g) polenta
½ cup (50g) pizza cheese
100g fetta cheese, crumbled

salsa
2 medium avocados (500g), chopped coarsely
⅔ cup (100g) drained semi-dried tomatoes in oil, chopped coarsely
1 lebanese cucumber (130g), chopped coarsely
1 small red capsicum (150g), chopped coarsely
⅓ cup coarsely chopped fresh flat-leaf parsley
½ teaspoon dried chilli flakes
¼ cup (60ml) red wine vinegar
¼ cup (60ml) olive oil

1 Grease 12-hole (⅓-cup/80ml) muffin pan.
2 Bring stock and the water to the boil in medium saucepan; gradually stir in polenta. Reduce heat; simmer, stirring, about 10 minutes or until polenta thickens. Stir in cheeses. Spoon polenta into muffin pan; smooth tops. Refrigerate 1 hour.
3 Preheat oven to 220°C/200°C fan-forced.
4 Bake polenta for 15 minutes. Gently turn polenta onto baking-paper-lined oven tray; bake about 5 minutes or until browned lightly.
5 Meanwhile, make salsa by combining ingredients in medium bowl.
6 Serve warm polenta, top-side up, topped with salsa.

preparation time *20 minutes (plus refrigeration time)*
cooking time *25 minutes* makes 12
nutritional count per polenta *15.2g total fat (4.2g saturated fat); 915kJ (219 cal); 13.7g carbohydrate; 6g protein; 2.4g fibre*

tip For a vegetarian option use vegetable stock.

CRAB, FENNEL AND HERB QUICHE

3 sheets ready-rolled shortcrust pastry
1 tablespoon olive oil
1 medium fennel bulb (300g), sliced thinly
250g crab meat
2 tablespoons finely chopped fennel fronds
2 tablespoons finely chopped fresh flat-leaf parsley
½ cup (60g) coarsely grated cheddar cheese

quiche filling
300ml cream
¼ cup (60ml) milk
3 eggs

1 Preheat oven to 200°C/180°C fan-forced. Grease 12-hole (⅓-cup/80ml) muffin pan.
2 Cut twelve 9cm rounds from pastry; press into pan holes.
3 Heat oil in large frying pan; cook fennel, stirring, about 5 minutes or until fennel softens and browns slightly. Divide fennel among pastry cases; top with combined crab, fronds, parsley and cheese.
4 Make quiche filling.
5 Pour quiche filling into pastry cases. Bake about 25 minutes. Stand in pan 5 minutes before serving with lime wedges.

quiche filling Whisk ingredients in large jug.
preparation time *20 minutes*
cooking time *30 minutes* makes *12*
nutritional count per quiche *27.1g total fat (15g saturated fat); 1509kJ (361 cal); 20.3g carbohydrate; 9g protein; 1.3g fibre*

tips We used lump crab meat from the fish market. Reserve fennel fronds when slicing the bulb.

thai chicken curry pies

fish chowder pies

THAI CHICKEN CURRY PIES

2 tablespoons peanut oil
1 medium brown onion (150g), sliced thinly
1 clove garlic, crushed
10cm stick fresh lemon grass (20g), chopped finely
2cm piece fresh ginger (10g), grated
600g chicken thigh fillets, cut into 3cm pieces
1 teaspoon ground cumin
½ teaspoon ground turmeric
165ml can coconut milk
1 tablespoon cornflour
¼ cup (60ml) chicken stock
1 tablespoon fish sauce
1 fresh kaffir lime leaf, shredded finely
1 fresh long red chilli, sliced thinly
¼ cup coarsely chopped fresh coriander
2 sheets ready-rolled shortcrust pastry
1 egg, beaten lightly
2 sheets ready-rolled puff pastry

1   Heat oil in large saucepan; cook onion, garlic, lemon grass and ginger, stirring, until onion softens. Add chicken; cook, stirring, until browned. Add spices; cook, stirring, until fragrant. Add coconut milk; bring to the boil. Reduce heat; simmer, uncovered, 10 minutes. Add blended cornflour and stock; cook, stirring, until mixture boils and thickens; cool. Stir in sauce, lime leaf, chilli and coriander.
2   Preheat oven to 200°C/180°C fan-forced. Grease six-hole (¾-cup/180ml) texas muffin pan.
3   Cut six 12cm rounds from shortcrust pastry; press into pan holes. Brush edges with a little of the egg. Divide chicken curry among pastry cases.
4   Cut six 9cm rounds from puff pastry; top chicken mixture with puff pastry rounds. Press edges firmly to seal. Brush tops with remaining egg. Cut a small slit in top of each pie.
5   Bake about 25 minutes. Stand pies in pan 5 minutes before serving, top-side up.

preparation time *25 minutes*
cooking time *50 minutes* makes *6*
nutritional count per pie *45.4g total fat (21.4g saturated fat); 3005kJ (719 cal); 49.6g carbohydrate; 27.7g protein; 2.3g fibre*

FISH CHOWDER PIES

40g butter
1 medium brown onion (150g), chopped coarsely
1 clove garlic, crushed
3 rindless bacon rashers (120g), chopped coarsely
2 tablespoons plain flour
1 cup (250ml) milk
½ cup (125ml) cream
2 small potatoes (240g), cut into 1cm pieces
600g firm white fish fillets, cut into 2cm pieces
¼ cup finely chopped fresh chives
2 sheets ready-rolled shortcrust pastry
1 egg, beaten lightly
2 sheets ready-rolled puff pastry

1   Melt butter in large saucepan; cook onion, garlic and bacon, stirring, until onion softens.
2   Add flour; cook, stirring, 1 minute. Gradually stir in combined milk and cream; bring to the boil. Add potato; simmer, covered, stirring occasionally, 8 minutes. Add fish; simmer, uncovered, 2 minutes; cool. Stir in chives.
3   Preheat oven to 200°C/180°C fan-forced. Grease six-hole (¾-cup/180ml) texas muffin pan.
4   Cut six 12cm rounds from shortcrust pastry; press into pan holes. Brush edges with a little of the egg. Divide fish chowder among pastry cases.
5   Cut six 9cm rounds from puff pastry; top chowder with puff pastry rounds. Press edges firmly to seal; brush tops with remaining egg. Cut a small slit in top of each pie.
6   Bake about 25 minutes. Stand pies in pan 5 minutes before serving, top-side up, sprinkled with chopped fresh chives.

preparation time *25 minutes*
cooking time *40 minutes* makes *6*
nutritional count per pie *49.8g total fat (27.4g saturated fat); 3415kJ (817 cal); 55.9g carbohydrate; 35.5g protein; 2.9g fibre*

FETTA AND SPINACH FILLO BUNDLES

350g spinach, trimmed
1 tablespoon olive oil
1 medium brown onion (150g), chopped finely
2 cloves garlic, crushed
½ teaspoon ground nutmeg
150g fetta cheese, crumbled
3 eggs
2 teaspoons finely grated lemon rind
¼ cup coarsely chopped fresh mint
2 tablespoons finely chopped fresh dill
80g butter, melted
6 sheets fillo pastry

1 Boil, steam or microwave spinach until wilted; drain. Refresh in cold water; drain. Squeeze out excess moisture. Chop spinach coarsely; spread out on absorbent paper.
2 Heat oil in small frying pan; cook onion and garlic, stirring, until onion softens. Add nutmeg; cook, stirring, until fragrant. Cool. Combine onion mixture and spinach in medium bowl with cheese, eggs, rind and herbs.
3 Preheat oven to 200°C/180°C fan-forced. Brush six-hole (¾-cup/180ml) texas muffin pan with a little of the butter.
4 Brush each sheet of fillo with melted butter; fold in half to enclose buttered side. Gently press one sheet into each pan hole.
5 Divide spinach mixture among pastry cases; fold fillo over filling to enclose. Brush with butter. Bake about 15 minutes. Turn fillo bundles out, top-side up, onto baking-paper-lined oven tray; bake about 5 minutes or until browned lightly. Stand 5 minutes before serving, top-side up.

preparation time *20 minutes*
cooking time *25 minutes* makes *6*
nutritional count per bundle *22.9g total fat*
(12.3g saturated fat); 1200kJ (287 cal);
9.6g carbohydrate; 10.4g protein; 1.8g fibre

LAMB MASALA PIES WITH RAITA

2 tablespoons vegetable oil
1 medium brown onion (150g), chopped finely
600g diced lamb
⅓ cup (100g) tikka masala paste
400g can diced tomatoes
¼ cup (60ml) water
½ cup (125ml) cream
¼ cup coarsely chopped fresh coriander
2 sheets ready-rolled shortcrust pastry
1 egg, beaten lightly
2 sheets ready-rolled puff pastry

raita
¾ cup (200g) yogurt
1 lebanese cucumber (130g), seeded, chopped finely
2 tablespoons finely chopped fresh mint

1 Heat oil in large saucepan; cook onion, stirring, until onion softens. Add lamb; cook, stirring, until browned. Add paste; cook, stirring, until fragrant. Add undrained tomatoes, the water and cream; bring to the boil. Reduce heat; simmer, uncovered, about 25 minutes or until sauce thickens; cool. Stir in coriander.
2 Preheat oven to 200°C/180°C fan-forced. Grease six-hole (¾-cup/180ml) texas muffin pan.
3 Cut six 12cm rounds from shortcrust pastry; press into pan holes. Brush edges with a little of the egg. Divide lamb curry among pastry cases.
4 Cut six 9cm rounds from puff pastry; top curry with puff pastry rounds. Press edges firmly to seal; brush tops with remaining egg. Cut a small slit in top of each pie.
5 Bake about 25 minutes. Stand pies in pan 5 minutes before serving.
6 Meanwhile, make raita by combining ingredients in small bowl.
7 Sprinkle lamb masala pies with fresh coriander leaves; serve with raita.

preparation time *25 minutes*
cooking time *1 hour* makes *6*
nutritional count per pie *54g total fat*
(24.7g saturated fat); 3469kJ (830 cal);
52g carbohydrate; 32.3g protein; 5.1g fibre

feta and spinach fillo bundles

lamb masala pies with raita

RISOTTO MILANESE TIMBALES WITH PESTO

2 cups (500ml) chicken stock
1½ cups (375ml) water
1 tablespoon olive oil
1 small brown onion (80g), chopped finely
1 clove garlic, crushed
1½ cups (300g) arborio rice
½ cup (125ml) dry white wine
pinch saffron threads
25g butter
½ cup (40g) coarsely grated parmesan cheese

pesto
1 cup firmly packed fresh basil leaves
2 tablespoons roasted pine nuts
1 clove garlic, quartered
2 tablespoons finely grated parmesan cheese
2 tablespoons olive oil
1 tablespoon lemon juice

1 Combine stock and the water in medium saucepan; bring to the boil. Reduce heat; simmer, covered.

2 Meanwhile, heat oil in large saucepan; cook onion and garlic, stirring, until onion softens. Add rice; stir to coat in onion mixture. Stir in wine and saffron; cook, stirring, until wine is absorbed. Add ½ cup of the simmering stock; cook, stirring, over low heat, until stock is absorbed. Continue adding stock, in ½ cup batches, stirring, until stock is absorbed after each addition. Total cooking time should be about 35 minutes or until rice is tender. Stir in butter and cheese. Cool to room temperature.

3 Grease six-hole (¾-cup/180ml) texas muffin pan; line with plastic wrap.

4 Make pesto.

5 Divide half the risotto among pan holes; top with pesto. Spoon remaining risotto over pesto; smooth tops. Refrigerate 3 hours. Remove timbales from refrigerator 1 hour before serving, top-side down.

pesto Process basil, nuts, garlic and cheese until chopped finely. With motor operating, gradually add combined oil and juice, in a thin, steady stream; process until pesto is smooth.

serving idea Accompany with grape tomatoes, sliced red onion and fresh basil leaves.

preparation time *25 minutes (plus refrigeration time)*
cooking time *40 minutes* makes 6
nutritional count per timbale *19.5g total fat*
(5.8g saturated fat); 1634kJ (391 cal);
41.5g carbohydrate; 8.7g protein; 1.2g fibre

PROSCIUTTO AND FETTA BAKED EGGS

12 slices prosciutto (180g)
¼ cup (35g) finely chopped drained
    semi-dried tomatoes in oil
50g fetta cheese, crumbled
2 tablespoons coarsely chopped fresh basil
2 tablespoons coarsely chopped fresh chives
6 eggs

1 Preheat oven to 200°C/180°C fan-forced. Grease six-hole (⅓-cup/80ml) muffin pan.
2 Wrap one prosciutto slice around edge of each pan hole, lay another slice to cover bases; press firmly to seal edges to form a cup. Divide half the combined tomato, cheese and herbs among prosciutto cups. Break an egg into each cup. Sprinkle with remaining cheese mixture.
3 Bake about 12 minutes or until eggs are cooked. Remove carefully from pan. Serve top-side up.
serving idea Accompany with cherry tomatoes.
preparation time *15 minutes*
cooking time *12 minutes* makes *6*
nutritional count per baked egg *9.4g total fat (3.6g saturated fat); 635kJ (152 cal); 2.3g carbohydrate; 14.3g protein; 0.9g fibre*

VEAL GOULASH PIES

600g diced veal shoulder
2 tablespoons plain flour
1 tablespoon sweet paprika
¼ teaspoon cayenne pepper
¼ cup (80ml) olive oil
1 small brown onion (80g), chopped finely
1 clove garlic, crushed
2 teaspoons caraway seeds
400g can diced tomatoes
¼ cup (60ml) beef stock
1 medium red capsicum (200g), cut into 2cm pieces
1 medium unpeeled potato (200g), cut into 2cm pieces
¼ cup (60g) sour cream
¼ cup coarsely chopped fresh flat-leaf parsley
2 sheets ready-rolled shortcrust pastry
1 egg, beaten lightly
2 sheets ready-rolled puff pastry

1 Coat veal in combined flour, paprika and pepper; shake off excess. Heat 2 tablespoons of the oil in large saucepan; cook veal, in batches, until browned.
2 Heat remaining oil in same pan; cook onion and garlic, stirring, until onion softens. Return veal to pan with seeds, undrained tomatoes and stock; bring to the boil. Reduce heat; simmer, covered, 25 minutes. Add capsicum and potato; simmer, uncovered, about 15 minutes or until sauce thickens. Stir in sour cream and parsley; cool.
3 Preheat oven to 200°C/180°C fan-forced. Grease six-hole (¾-cup/180ml) texas muffin pan.
4 Cut six 12cm rounds from shortcrust pastry; press into pan holes. Brush edges with a little of the egg. Divide goulash among pastry cases.
5 Cut six 9cm rounds from puff pastry; top goulash with puff pastry rounds. Press edges firmly to seal; brush tops with remaining egg. Cut a small slit in top of each pie.
6 Bake about 25 minutes. Stand pies in pan 5 minutes before serving, top-side up.
preparation time *25 minutes*
cooking time *1 hour 15 minutes* makes *6*
nutritional count per pie *44.6g total fat (19.7g saturated fat); 3198kJ (765 cal); 56g carbohydrate; 33.3g protein; 4.1g fibre*

prosciutto and fetta baked eggs

veal goulash pies

meat pie scrolls

salmon and potato soufflés

MEAT PIE SCROLLS

1 tablespoon olive oil
1 small brown onion (80g), chopped finely
1 clove garlic, crushed
3 rindless bacon rashers (120g), chopped finely
300g beef mince
400g can diced tomatoes
1 tablespoon tomato paste
2 tablespoons worcestershire sauce
½ cup (125ml) beef stock
¼ cup coarsely chopped fresh flat-leaf parsley
2 cups (300g) self-raising flour
1 tablespoon caster sugar
50g butter, chopped coarsely
¾ cup (180ml) milk
1 cup (110g) pizza cheese

1 Heat oil in large frying pan; cook onion, garlic and
bacon, stirring, until onion softens. Add beef; cook, stirring,
until beef changes colour. Add undrained tomatoes, paste,
sauce and stock; bring to the boil. Reduce heat; simmer,
uncovered, about 20 minutes or until sauce thickens.
Remove from heat; stir in parsley. Cool.
2 Preheat oven to 180°C/160°C fan-forced. Grease
two six-hole (¾-cup/180ml) texas muffin pans.
3 Sift flour and sugar into medium bowl; rub in butter
with fingers. Stir in milk; mix to a soft, sticky dough.
Knead dough on floured surface; roll dough out to
30cm x 40cm rectangle.
4 Spread beef mixture over dough; sprinkle with cheese.
Roll dough tightly from one long side; trim ends. Cut roll
into 12 slices; place one slice in each pan hole. Bake
about 25 minutes. Serve top-side up.

preparation time *25 minutes*
cooking time *50 minutes* makes *12*
nutritional count per scroll *11g total fat*
(5.4g saturated fat); 1024kJ (245 cal);
22.3g carbohydrate; 13.3g protein; 1.6g fibre

SALMON AND POTATO SOUFFLÉS

300g potatoes, chopped coarsely
300g salmon fillets
2 tablespoons packaged breadcrumbs
50g butter
1 small brown onion (80g), chopped finely
2 tablespoons plain flour
¾ cup (180ml) milk
2 egg yolks
3 eggs whites
¼ cup (20g) finely grated parmesan cheese
2 tablespoons finely chopped garlic chives
1 teaspoon finely grated lemon rind

1 Boil, steam or microwave potato until tender; drain.
Mash until smooth.
2 Meanwhile, cook fish in medium saucepan of
simmering water, uncovered, about 4 minutes or until
cooked. When cool enough to handle, flake fish.
3 Preheat oven to 220°C/200°C fan-forced. Grease
six-hole (¾-cup/180ml) texas muffin pan.
4 Divide breadcrumbs among pan holes; shake pan
to coat bases and sides with breadcrumbs. Place pan
on oven tray.
5 Melt butter in medium saucepan; cook onion, stirring,
until onion softens. Add flour; cook, stirring, until mixture
thickens and bubbles. Gradually stir in milk; cook, stirring,
until mixture boils and thickens. Transfer mixture to large
bowl; stir in egg yolks, cheese, chives, rind, potato
and salmon.
6 Beat egg whites in small bowl with electric mixer
until soft peaks form. Fold egg whites into salmon mixture,
in two batches. Divide soufflé mixture among pan holes.
Bake about 20 minutes.
7 Gently turn soufflés out; serve immediately, top-side up.

serving ideas Accompany with lemon wedges and
sour cream.

preparation time *15 minutes*
cooking time *30 minutes* makes *6*
nutritional count per soufflé *14.7g total fat*
(7.4g saturated fat); 1045kJ (250 cal);
12.2g carbohydrate; 16.9g protein; 1.1g fibre

NACHOS

1 tablespoon olive oil
1 small brown onion (80g), chopped finely
1 clove garlic, crushed
400g beef mince
1 fresh long red chilli, chopped finely
35g packet taco seasoning mix
400g can diced tomatoes
1 tablespoon tomato paste
⅓ cup (80ml) beef stock
420g can mexican chilli beans, rinsed, drained
¼ cup coarsely chopped fresh coriander
230g corn chips, chopped coarsely
1½ cups (180g) coarsely grated cheddar cheese

guacamole
1 large avocado (320g), chopped coarsely
1 medium tomato (150g), chopped finely
½ small red onion (50g), chopped finely
1 tablespoon lime juice
1 tablespoon finely chopped fresh coriander

1 Heat oil in large frying pan; cook onion and garlic, stirring, until onion softens. Add beef; cook, stirring, until beef changes colour. Add chilli and seasoning mix; cook, stirring, until fragrant.

2 Add undrained tomatoes, paste and stock; bring to the boil. Reduce heat; simmer, uncovered, 15 minutes. Add beans; cook, stirring, about 5 minutes or until thickened. Stir in coriander. Cool.

3 Preheat oven to 200°C/180°C fan-forced. Grease eight holes of two 6-hole (¾-cup/180ml) texas muffin pans; line greased pan holes with two criss-crossed 5cm x 20cm strips of baking paper.

4 Combine corn chips and 1 cup of the cheese in small bowl; divide half the corn chip mixture among pan holes, pressing down firmly. Divide beef mixture among pan holes; top with remaining corn chip mixture, pressing down firmly. Sprinkle with remaining cheese. Bake about 15 minutes or until browned lightly.

5 Meanwhile, make guacamole by mashing avocado in medium bowl; stir in remaining ingredients.

6 Stand nachos in pan 5 minutes. Using baking paper strips as lifters, carefully remove nachos from pan holes. Serve topped with guacamole; sprinkle with fresh coriander leaves.

serving idea Accompany with lime wedges and sour cream.

preparation time *20 minutes*
cooking time *45 minutes* makes *8*
nutritional count per nacho *27.7g total fat (11g saturated fat); 1839kJ (440 cal); 23.1g carbohydrate; 21.9g protein; 6.9g fibre*

spinach and three cheese muffins

pumpkin and fetta muffins

SPINACH AND THREE CHEESE MUFFINS

2 tablespoons olive oil
1 small brown onion (80g), chopped finely
100g baby spinach leaves
½ cup (50g) coarsely grated mozzarella cheese
½ cup (40g) coarsely grated parmesan cheese
100g blue cheese, crumbled
1 quantity basic muffin mix *(see pizza muffins recipe, page 13)*

1   Preheat oven to 200°C/180°C fan-forced. Grease 12-hole (⅓-cup/80ml) muffin pan.
2   Heat oil in medium frying pan; cook onion, stirring, until onion softens. Add spinach; cook, stirring, about 1 minute or until wilted. Cool.
3   Combine cheeses and spinach mixture in large bowl with basic muffin mix. Do not over-mix; mixture should be lumpy.
4   Divide mixture among pan holes. Bake about 20 minutes. Stand muffins 5 minutes before turning, top-side up, onto wire rack. Serve muffins warm.
preparation time *20 minutes*
cooking time *25 minutes* makes *12*
nutritional count per muffin *14.6g total fat (7.5g saturated fat); 1007kJ (241 cal); 17.1g carbohydrate; 8.9g protein; 3.1g fibre*

PUMPKIN AND FETTA MUFFINS

1 tablespoon olive oil
200g piece pumpkin, cut into 1cm pieces
1 clove garlic, crushed
50g fetta cheese, crumbled
¼ cup (20g) finely grated parmesan cheese
¼ cup finely chopped fresh chives
1 quantity basic muffin mix *(see pizza muffins recipe, page 13)*

1   Preheat oven to 200°C/180°C fan-forced. Grease 12-hole (⅓-cup/80ml) muffin pan.
2   Heat oil in small frying pan; cook pumpkin, stirring, about 5 minutes or until tender. Add garlic; cook, stirring, 1 minute. Cool.
3   Combine cheeses, chives and pumpkin mixture in medium bowl with basic muffin mix. Do not over-mix; mixture should be lumpy.
4   Divide mixture among pan holes. Bake about 20 minutes. Stand muffins 5 minutes before turning, top-side up, onto wire rack. Serve muffins warm.
serving idea Accompany warm muffins with butter.
preparation time *20 minutes*
cooking time *25 minutes* makes *12*
nutritional count per muffin *10g total fat (5.3g saturated fat); 803kJ (192 cal); 7.7g carbohydrate; 6.3g protein; 3.1g fibre*

SMOKED SALMON AND CREAM CHEESE STACKS

250g cream cheese, softened
½ cup (120g) sour cream
2 tablespoons lemon juice
2 tablespoons finely chopped fresh dill
2 teaspoons coarsely chopped baby capers
1 teaspoon finely grated lemon rind
300g sliced smoked salmon

1   Grease six-hole (⅓-cup/80ml) muffin pan; line with plastic wrap.
2   Beat cheese, sour cream and juice in small bowl with electric mixer until smooth. Stir in dill, capers and rind.
3   Cut twelve 6cm rounds and twelve 7cm rounds from salmon slices. Place one small salmon round in base of each pan hole; top with 1 tablespoon of cream-cheese mixture. Layer with remaining small salmon rounds and another 1 tablespoon of cream-cheese mixture. Repeat with larger rounds and remaining cream-cheese, finishing with salmon.
4   Cover pan with plastic wrap; refrigerate 1 hour. Remove stacks from pan; carefully remove plastic wrap. Serve salmon stacks, top-side down.
serving idea   Rocket salad and lime wedges.
preparation time *30 minutes (plus refrigeration time)*
makes *6*
nutritional count per stack   *24g total fat (14.5g saturated fat); 1187kJ (284 cal); 2g carbohydrate; 15.6g protein; 0g fibre*

tip   If salmon slices are less than 7cm wide, you may need to join two pieces together before cutting out rounds. Do this by slightly overlapping edges of salmon, then press down.

CARAMELISED LEEK AND BRIE TARTLETS

1 tablespoon olive oil
25g butter
2 medium leeks (700g), sliced finely
1 clove garlic, crushed
1 tablespoon brown sugar
1 tablespoon white wine vinegar
3 sheets ready-rolled puff pastry
200g piece brie cheese
24 sprigs lemon thyme

1   Preheat oven to 200°C/180°C fan-forced. Grease two 12-hole (2-tablespoons/40ml) deep flat-based patty pans.
2   Heat oil and butter in large frying pan; cook leek over medium heat, stirring, about 5 minutes or until leek softens. Add garlic, sugar and vinegar; cook, stirring, about 8 minutes or until leek caramelises.
3   Cut 8 squares from each pastry sheet; press one pastry square into each pan hole. Divide leek mixture among pastry cases.
4   Cut cheese into 24 slices. Place a slice of cheese and thyme sprig on top of each tartlet. Bake about 20 minutes.
preparation time *10 minutes*
cooking time *30 minutes*   makes *24*
nutritional count per tartlet   *8.8g total fat (4.8g saturated fat); 535kJ (128 cal); 8.7g carbohydrate; 3.1g protein; 0.8g fibre*

tip   To make the squares, we used an 8.5cm square cutter, measuring 8.5cm from corner to corner.

smoked salmon and cream cheese stacks

caramelised leek and brie tartlets

PUMPKIN AND GOATS CHEESE LASAGNE

700g piece butternut pumpkin, peeled
1 tablespoon olive oil
3 fresh lasagne sheets (150g)
150g baby spinach leaves
120g goats cheese, chopped finely
¼ cup (20g) finely grated parmesan cheese

white sauce
20g butter
1 tablespoon plain flour
1½ cups (375ml) milk
¼ cup (20g) finely grated parmesan cheese

1 Preheat oven to 200°C/180°C fan-forced. Grease six-hole (¾-cup/180ml) texas muffin pan; line each pan hole with two criss-crossed 5cm x 20cm strips of baking paper.
2 Cut pumpkin lengthways into 1cm-thick slices. Cut six 7cm rounds and six 8cm rounds from pumpkin slices. Brush pumpkin rounds with oil; place in large baking dish in a single layer. Roast about 15 minutes or until tender.
3 Meanwhile, cut six 7cm rounds and twelve 8cm rounds from lasagne sheets.
4 Make white sauce.
5 Boil, steam or microwave spinach until wilted; drain. Refresh in cold water; drain. Squeeze out excess moisture. Chop spinach coarsely; spread out on absorbent paper.
6 Divide a third of the white sauce among pan holes; place one small pasta round in each hole; top with half the goats cheese, half the spinach then a small pumpkin round. Repeat layers with another third of the sauce, six large pasta rounds and remaining goats cheese, spinach and pumpkin. Top lasagne stacks with remaining pasta rounds and white sauce; sprinkle with parmesan.
7 Bake about 25 minutes or until browned lightly. Stand lasagne in pan 5 minutes. Using baking paper strips as lifters, carefully remove lasagne from pan holes. Serve top-side up.
white sauce Melt butter in medium saucepan, add flour; cook, stirring, 1 minute. Gradually stir in milk; cook, stirring, until sauce boils and thickens. Stir in cheese.
preparation time *25 minutes*
cooking time *45 minutes* makes 6
nutritional count per stack *14.1g total fat (7.6g saturated fat); 1016kJ (243 cal); 17g carbohydrate; 11.1g protein; 2.3g fibre*

MEATLOAVES WITH BARBECUE GLAZE

16 slices prosciutto (240g)
500g beef mince
350g veal mince
1 small brown onion (80g), chopped finely
4 slices (170g) bottled roasted capsicum, chopped finely
2 cloves garlic, crushed
1 egg
2 tablespoons barbecue sauce
⅓ cup (25g) stale breadcrumbs
1 tablespoon finely chopped fresh oregano

barbecue glaze
¼ cup (60ml) barbecue sauce
2 tablespoons tomato sauce
1 tablespoon lemon juice
1 tablespoon brown sugar

1 Preheat oven to 200°C/180°C fan-forced.
2 Grease eight-hole (½-cup/125ml) petite loaf pan. Line each pan hole with two criss-crossed slices of prosciutto, extending above edges of holes.
3 Make barbecue glaze by combining ingredients in small saucepan; stir over low heat until sugar dissolves.
4 Combine minces, onion, capsicum, garlic, egg, sauce, breadcrumbs and oregano in large bowl. Press meatloaf mixture into pan holes; fold prosciutto over to enclose meat mixture.
5 Bake 15 minutes; turn, top-side down, onto baking-paper-lined oven tray. Brush meatloaves with glaze; bake, uncovered, 10 minutes or until browned lightly and cooked through. Serve top-side down.
serving idea Rocket and tomato salad.
preparation time *20 minutes*
cooking time *35 minutes* makes *8*
nutritional count per meatloaf *11.4g total fat (4g saturated fat); 1137kJ (272 cal); 12.3g carbohydrate; 29.6g protein; 0.6g fibre*

CHICKEN MEATLOAVES WITH SALSA VERDE

900g chicken mince
⅔ cup (100g) drained semi-dried tomatoes in oil, chopped finely
2 cloves garlic, crushed
1 egg
⅓ cup (25g) stale breadcrumbs
¼ cup (40g) roasted pine nuts
¼ cup coarsely chopped fresh chives

salsa verde
½ cup coarsely chopped fresh flat-leaf parsley
¼ cup coarsely chopped fresh dill
¼ cup coarsely chopped fresh chives
1 tablespoon rinsed, drained baby capers, chopped coarsely
⅓ cup (80ml) olive oil
¼ cup (60ml) lemon juice
1 tablespoon wholegrain mustard
1 clove garlic, crushed

1 Preheat oven to 200°C/180°C fan-forced. Grease eight-hole (½-cup/125ml) petite loaf pan.
2 Make salsa verde.
3 Combine chicken, tomato, garlic, egg, breadcrumbs, nuts and chives in large bowl. Press meatloaf mixture into pan holes.
4 Bake 10 minutes; turn onto baking-paper-lined oven tray. Bake about 10 minutes or until browned lightly and cooked through.
5 Serve meatloaves, top-side up, with salsa verde.
salsa verde Combine ingredients in small bowl.
serving idea Accompany with toasted crusty bread.
preparation time *15 minutes*
cooking time *20 minutes* makes *8*
nutritional count per meatloaf *23.6g total fat (4.5g saturated fat); 1442kJ (345 cal); 7.3g carbohydrate; 25.2g protein; 2.7g fibre*

tip We used chicken breast mince in this recipe.

meatloaves with barbecue glaze

chicken meatloaves with salsa verde

goats cheese and zucchini flower quiche

prosciutto and roasted capsicum quiche

GOATS CHEESE AND ZUCCHINI FLOWER QUICHE

12 baby zucchini with flowers (240g)
3 sheets ready-rolled shortcrust pastry
100g firm goats cheese, chopped finely
⅓ cup (25g) finely grated parmesan cheese
2 tablespoons finely chopped garlic chives
1 quantity quiche filling (see crab, fennel and
   herb quiche recipe, page 26)

1 Preheat oven to 200°C/180°C fan-forced. Grease
12-hole (⅓-cup/80ml) muffin pan.
2 Remove flowers from zucchini; remove and discard
stamens from flowers. Slice zucchini thinly.
3 Cut twelve 9cm rounds from pastry; press into pan
holes. Divide combined sliced zucchini, cheeses and
chives into pastry cases; pour quiche filling into pastry
cases. Top each quiche with a zucchini flower.
4 Bake about 25 minutes. Stand in pan 5 minutes
before serving.
preparation time *25 minutes*
cooking time *25 minutes* makes *12*
nutritional count per quiche *25.8g total fat*
(15g saturated fat); 1421kJ (340 cal);
19.9g carbohydrate; 7.1g protein; 1.1g fibre

PROSCIUTTO AND ROASTED CAPSICUM QUICHE

6 slices prosciutto (90g)
3 sheets ready-rolled shortcrust pastry
4 slices (170g) bottled roasted red capsicum,
   chopped coarsely
⅓ cup coarsely chopped fresh basil
¾ cup (75g) pizza cheese
1 quantity quiche filling (see crab, fennel and
   herb quiche recipe, page 26)

1 Preheat oven to 200°C/180°C fan-forced. Grease
12-hole (⅓-cup/80ml) muffin pan.
2 Cook prosciutto in heated oiled large frying pan until
crisp. Cool; chop coarsely.
3 Cut twelve 9cm rounds from pastry; press into pan
holes. Divide combined prosciutto, capsicum, basil
and cheese among pastry cases; pour quiche filling
into pastry cases.
4 Bake about 25 minutes. Stand in pan 5 minutes
before serving.
preparation time *20 minutes*
cooking time *30 minutes* makes *12*
nutritional count per quiche *26.5g total fat*
(14.8g saturated fat); 1462kJ (350 cal);
19.7g carbohydrate; 8.3g protein; 0.8g fibre

VIETNAMESE CHICKEN WONTON CUPS

18 wonton wrappers
cooking-oil spray
2 cups (320g) shredded barbecued chicken
1 small carrot (70g), cut into matchsticks
1 small red capsicum (150g), cut into matchsticks
2 cups (160g) finely shredded wombok
1 cup (80g) bean sprouts
¼ cup coarsely chopped vietnamese mint leaves
¼ cup coarsely chopped fresh coriander
¼ cup (35g) coarsely chopped raw unsalted peanuts
2 tablespoons fried shallots

vietnamese dressing
¼ cup (60ml) lime juice
2 tablespoons fish sauce
1 tablespoon caster sugar
1 tablespoon water
2 teaspoons sesame oil

1   Preheat oven to 220°C/200°C fan-forced. Grease six-hole (¾-cup/180ml) texas muffin pan.
2   Spray wonton wrappers with oil; line each pan hole with three wrappers, oil-side up, overlapping slightly to form cups. Bake about 7 minutes or until browned lightly and crisp.
3   Meanwhile, make vietnamese dressing by placing ingredients in screw-top jar; shake well.
4   Combine chicken, carrot, capsicum, wombok, sprouts, herbs, nuts and dressing in large bowl.
5   Divide chicken salad among wonton cups; sprinkle with fried shallots.
preparation time *20 minutes*
cooking time *7 minutes* makes *6*
nutritional count per wonton cup   *10g total fat (1.9g saturated fat); 832kJ (199 cal); 7g carbohydrate; 19.2g protein; 2.2g fibre*

THAI PRAWN AND PAPAYA RICE PAPER PARCELS

750g cooked large prawns
6 green onions
1 small green papaya (650g), peeled, cut into matchsticks
1 cup (80g) bean sprouts
2 fresh long red chillies, sliced thinly
⅓ cup coarsely chopped fresh coriander
6 x 22cm-round rice-paper sheets

thai dressing
¼ cup (60ml) lime juice
2 tablespoons fish sauce
2 tablespoons peanut oil
1 tablespoon grated palm sugar
1 clove garlic, crushed

1   Shell and devein prawns; chop meat coarsely. Remove white part from green onions, chop finely and reserve. Cut green part of each onion into two long strips; submerge in hot water for a few seconds to make pliable.
2   Make thai dressing by placing ingredients in screw-top jar; shake well.
3   Combine papaya, sprouts, chilli, coriander, dressing, prawn meat and reserved chopped onion in large bowl.
4   Line each hole of six-hole (¾-cup/180ml) texas muffin pan with two criss-crossed green onion strips, extending 5cm above edge of holes.
5   Dip rice-paper sheets, one at a time, in medium bowl of warm water until softened; gently press on dry tea towel to absorb excess moisture. Carefully press one sheet into each pan hole to cover onion strips.
6   Drain excess dressing from salad into small jug; reserve. Divide salad among rice-paper cups; fold rice paper over to enclose salad. Gently pull green onion strips over centre of parcel; tie ends to secure.
7   Carefully remove rice paper parcels from pan; serve with reserved dressing, sprinkle with fresh coriander leaves.
preparation time *25 minutes* makes *6*
nutritional count per parcel   *6.7g total fat (1.2g saturated fat); 711kJ (170 cal); 11.7g carbohydrate; 14.2g protein; 2.8g fibre*

vietnamese chicken wonton cups

thai prawn and papaya rice paper parcels

MUFFINS

APPLE STREUSEL MUFFINS

40g butter
3 large apples (600g), peeled, cut into 1cm pieces
⅓ cup (75g) firmly packed brown sugar
2 cups (300g) self-raising flour
1 teaspoon mixed spice
⅔ cup (150g) caster sugar
80g butter, melted, extra
¾ cup (180ml) buttermilk
1 egg

streusel topping
⅓ cup (50g) self-raising flour
⅓ cup (50g) plain flour
⅓ cup (75g) firmly packed brown sugar
½ teaspoon ground cinnamon
80g cold butter, chopped coarsely

1 Make streusel topping.
2 Meanwhile, melt butter in large frying pan; cook apple, stirring, about 5 minutes or until browned lightly. Add brown sugar; cook, stirring, about 5 minutes or until mixture thickens. Cool.
3 Preheat oven to 200°C/180°C fan-forced. Line 12-hole (⅓-cup/80ml) muffin pan with paper cases.
4 Sift flour, spice and sugar into large bowl. Stir in the combined extra butter, buttermilk and egg. Do not over-mix; mixture should be lumpy. Stir in half the apple mixture.
5 Divide mixture among pan holes; top with remaining apple mixture.
6 Coarsely grate streusel topping over muffin mixture. Bake about 20 minutes. Stand muffins 5 minutes before turning, top-side up, onto wire rack to cool.
streusel topping Process flours, sugar and cinnamon until combined. Add butter; process until combined. Roll dough into ball, wrap in plastic wrap; freeze about 15 minutes or until firm.
preparation time *20 minutes (plus freezing time)*
cooking time *20 minutes* makes *12*
nutritional count per muffin *14.2g total fat (9g saturated fat); 1471kJ (352 cal); 50.4g carbohydrate; 4.6g protein; 1.9g fibre*

tips Store muffins in an airtight container for up to two days. We used freeform paper cases made by pushing a 12cm square of paper (we used paper about the same thickness as printer paper) into ungreased pan holes, followed by a 12cm square of baking paper.

DATE MUFFINS WITH ORANGE SYRUP

1¼ cups (185g) white self-raising flour
1 cup (160g) wholemeal self-raising flour
1 cup (220g) caster sugar
100g butter, melted
1 cup (280g) yogurt
2 eggs
1 teaspoon finely grated orange rind
1½ cups (210g) coarsely chopped seeded dried dates

orange syrup
½ cup (110g) caster sugar
¼ cup (60ml) water
2 teaspoons finely grated orange rind
¼ cup (60ml) orange juice

1 Preheat oven to 200°C/180°C fan-forced. Grease 12-hole (⅓-cup/80ml) muffin pan with butter.
2 Sift flours and sugar into large bowl. Stir in combined butter, yogurt, eggs and rind. Do not over-mix; mixture should be lumpy. Stir in dates. Divide mixture among pan holes. Bake about 20 minutes.
3 Meanwhile, make orange syrup.
4 Stand muffins 2 minutes before turning, top-side up, onto wire rack. Stand rack over tray. Pierce muffins all over with skewer; pour hot orange syrup over hot muffins.
orange syrup Stir ingredients in small saucepan over heat until sugar dissolves. Bring to the boil; reduce heat. Simmer, uncovered, 2 minutes.

preparation time *15 minutes*
cooking time *20 minutes* makes *12*
nutritional count per muffin *9g total fat
(5.4g saturated fat); 1480kJ (354 cal);
60g carbohydrate; 5.8g protein; 3.8g fibre*

tip Store muffins in an airtight container for up to two days.

variation
fig muffins with orange syrup Omit the dates and replace with 1 cup coarsely chopped dried figs.

BANANA, CRANBERRY AND MACADAMIA MUFFINS

2¼ cups (335g) self-raising flour
¾ cup (165g) caster sugar
½ cup (65g) dried cranberries
½ cup (70g) coarsely chopped roasted
   unsalted macadamias
⅔ cup mashed banana
2 eggs, beaten lightly
1 cup (250ml) milk
½ cup (125ml) vegetable oil

1 Preheat oven to 200°C/180°C fan-forced. Line three six-hole (⅓-cup/80ml) muffin pans with paper cases.
2 Sift flour and sugar into large bowl; stir in berries and nuts. Stir in the combined remaining ingredients; do not over-mix, mixture should be lumpy.
3 Divide mixture among pan holes. Bake about 20 minutes. Stand muffins 5 minutes before turning, top-side up, onto wire rack to cool. Serve lightly dusted with sifted icing sugar.
preparation time *10 minutes*
cooking time *20 minutes* makes *18*
nutritional count per muffin *10.7g total fat*
(18g saturated fat); 933kJ (223 cal);
27.5g carbohydrate; 3.6g protein; 1.3g fibre

tips Store muffins in an airtight container for up to two days. You need two medium (400g) overripe bananas to get the required amount of mashed banana.
We used freeform paper cases made by pushing a 12cm square of paper (we used paper about the same thickness as printer paper) into ungreased pan holes, followed by a 12cm square of baking paper.

variation
banana, raisin and pecan muffins Omit the cranberries and replace with ½ cup coarsely chopped raisins. Omit the macadamias and replace with ½ cup coarsely chopped roasted pecans.

GINGER AND PEAR MUFFINS

2 cups (300g) self-raising flour
1 teaspoon ground ginger
¾ cup (165g) caster sugar
80g butter, melted
1 cup (280g) yogurt
2 eggs
2 medium pears (460g), peeled, chopped finely

muesli topping
50g butter
2 tablespoons honey
2 cups (220g) natural muesli

1 Preheat oven to 200°C/180°C fan-forced. Line 12-hole (⅓-cup/80ml) muffin pan with paper cases.
2 Make muesli topping.
3 Sift flour and ginger into large bowl; stir in sugar and the combined butter, yogurt and eggs. Do not over-mix; mixture should be lumpy. Gently stir in pears.
4 Spoon mixture into pan holes; spoon muesli topping onto muffin mixture. Bake about 20 minutes. Stand muffins 5 minutes before turning, top-side up, onto wire rack to cool.
muesli topping Stir butter and honey in small saucepan over low heat until combined. Remove from heat; stir in muesli.
preparation time *15 minutes*
cooking time *20 minutes* makes *12*
nutritional count per muffin *12.5g total fat*
(7.1g saturated fat); 1471kJ (352 cal);
51g carbohydrate; 6.7g protein; 3.3g fibre

tips Buy a muesli that contains dried fruit to add colour and flavour to the muffins.
Store muffins in an airtight container for up to two days. We used freeform paper cases made by pushing a 12cm square of paper (we used paper about the same thickness as printer paper) into ungreased pan holes, followed by a 12cm square of baking paper.

banana, cranberry and macadamia muffins

ginger and pear muffins

butterscotch pecan muffins

chocolate raspberry dessert muffins

BUTTERSCOTCH PECAN MUFFINS

¾ cup (240g) Nestlé Top n' Fill Caramel
2 cups (300g) self-raising flour
¾ cup (165g) firmly packed brown sugar
¾ cup (90g) coarsely chopped roasted pecans
80g butter, melted
1 cup (250ml) buttermilk
1 egg

1 Preheat oven to 200°C/180°C fan-forced. Line 12-hole (⅓-cup/80ml) muffin pan with paper cases.
2 Stir caramel in small saucepan over low heat until smooth. Cool 5 minutes.
3 Meanwhile sift flour and sugar into large bowl. Stir in nuts and the combined butter, buttermilk and egg. Do not over-mix; mixture should be lumpy.
4 Divide half the mixture among paper cases. Spoon half the caramel over muffin mixture; top with remaining mixture then caramel. Using a skewer, gently swirl caramel into muffin mixture. Bake about 20 minutes. Stand muffins 5 minutes before turning, top-side up, onto wire rack to cool.

preparation time *15 minutes*
cooking time *25 minutes* makes *12*
nutritional count per muffin *13.4g total fat*
(5.4g saturated fat); 1325kJ (317 cal);
33.5g carbohydrate; 6g protein; 1.6g fibre

tip Store muffins in an airtight container for up to two days.

CHOCOLATE RASPBERRY DESSERT MUFFINS

1¾ cups (260g) self-raising flour
¼ cup (25g) cocoa powder
¾ cup (165g) caster sugar
50g butter, melted
⅔ cup (160ml) milk
½ cup (120g) sour cream
2 eggs
½ cup (70g) coarsely chopped roasted hazelnuts
150g dark eating chocolate, chopped coarsely
1 cup (150g) frozen raspberries

1 Preheat oven to 200°C/180°C fan-forced. Line 12-hole (⅓-cup/80ml) muffin pan with paper cases.
2 Sift flour, cocoa and sugar into large bowl. Stir in the combined butter, milk, sour cream and eggs. Do not over-mix; mixture should be lumpy. Stir in remaining ingredients.
3 Divide mixture among paper cases. Bake about 20 minutes. Stand muffins 5 minutes before turning, top-side up, onto wire rack to cool.

preparation time *15 minutes*
cooking time *20 minutes* makes *12*
nutritional count per muffin *15.6g total fat*
(8g saturated fat); 1400kJ (335 cal);
39.4g carbohydrate; 6g protein; 2.4g fibre

tips These muffins are best served warm.
Store muffins in an airtight container for up to two days.
We used freeform paper cases made by pushing a 12cm square of paper (we used paper about the same thickness as printer paper) into ungreased pan holes, followed by a 12cm square of baking paper.

RHUBARB AND CUSTARD MUFFINS

2 cups (300g) self-raising flour
½ cup (75g) plain flour
¾ cup (165g) caster sugar
100g butter, melted
1 cup (250ml) milk
1 egg
3 cups (330g) finely chopped rhubarb
1 tablespoon demerara sugar

custard
2 tablespoons custard powder
¼ cup (55g) caster sugar
1 cup (250ml) milk
1 teaspoon vanilla extract

1 Make custard.
2 Preheat oven to 200°C/180°C fan-forced. Line 12-hole (⅓-cup/80ml) muffin pan with paper cases.
3 Sift flours and caster sugar into large bowl. Stir in the combined butter, milk and egg. Do not over-mix; mixture should be lumpy. Stir in half the rhubarb.
4 Divide half the mixture among paper cases; top with custard. Divide remaining mixture over custard. Sprinkle with remaining rhubarb and demerara sugar.
5 Bake about 25 minutes. Stand muffins 5 minutes before turning, top-side up, onto wire rack to cool. Serve lightly dusted with sifted icing sugar.
custard Combine custard powder and sugar in small saucepan; gradually stir in milk. Stir mixture over medium heat until custard boils and thickens. Stir in extract; cool.
preparation time *20 minutes*
cooking time *30 minutes* makes *12*
nutritional count per muffin *9.3g total fat*
(5.8g saturated fat); 1233kJ (295 cal);
45.7g carbohydrate; 5.7g protein; 1.9g fibre

tips You need five large stems of rhubarb to get the required amount of chopped rhubarb.
Store muffins in an airtight container for up to two days.

BERRY BUTTERMILK MUFFINS

2½ cups (375g) self-raising flour
100g butter, chopped coarsely
1 cup (220g) caster sugar
1¼ cups (310ml) buttermilk
1 egg, beaten lightly
1⅓ cups (200g) frozen mixed berries

1 Preheat oven to 200°C/180°C fan-forced. Line 12-hole (⅓-cup/80ml) muffin pan with paper cases.
2 Sift flour into large bowl; rub in butter using fingers. Stir in sugar, buttermilk and egg. Do not over-mix; mixture should be lumpy. Stir in berries.
3 Divide mixture among pan holes. Bake, uncovered, about 20 minutes. Stand muffins 5 minutes before turning, top-side up, onto wire rack to cool.
preparation time *10 minutes*
cooking time *20 minutes* makes *12*
nutritional count per muffin *8.2g total fat*
(5g saturated fat); 1120kJ (268 cal);
42.4g carbohydrate; 5.1g protein; 1.6g fibre

tips This recipe works well with any type of frozen or fresh berries.
Store muffins in an airtight container for up to two days.

variation
mango buttermilk muffins Omit the raspberries and replace with 1 small finely chopped mango (300g).

rhubarb and custard muffins

berry buttermilk muffins

CUPCAKES

PASSIONFRUIT CURD SPONGE CAKES

3 eggs
½ cup (110g) caster sugar
¾ cup (110g) self-raising flour
20g butter
¼ cup (60ml) boiling water

passionfruit curd
⅓ cup (80ml) passionfruit pulp
½ cup (110g) caster sugar
2 eggs, beaten lightly
125g unsalted butter, chopped coarsely

1 Make passionfruit curd.
2 Preheat oven to 180°C/160°C fan-forced. Grease 12-hole (½-cup/125ml) oval friand pan with softened butter; dust lightly with flour.
3 Beat eggs in small bowl with electric mixer until thick and creamy. Gradually add sugar, beating until dissolved between additions. Transfer mixture to large bowl. Fold in sifted flour then combined butter and the boiling water.
4 Divide mixture among pan holes. Bake about 12 minutes. Working quickly, loosen edges of cakes from pan using a small knife; turn immediately onto baking-paper-covered wire racks to cool.
5 Split cooled cakes in half. Spread cut-sides with curd; replace tops. Serve lightly dusted with sifted icing sugar.
passionfruit curd Combine ingredients in medium heatproof bowl; stir over pan of simmering water about 10 minutes or until mixture coats the back of a wooden spoon. Cover; refrigerate 3 hours.
preparation time *25 minutes (plus refrigeration and cooling time)*
cooking time *12 minutes* makes *12*
nutritional count per cake *12.2g total fat (7.2g saturated fat); 957kJ (229 cal); 25.3g carbohydrate; 3.9g protein; 1.2g fibre*

tip You need four passionfruit to get the required amount of passionfruit pulp needed for this recipe.

PATTY CAKES WITH GLACE ICING

125g butter, softened
½ teaspoon vanilla extract
¾ cup (165g) caster sugar
3 eggs
2 cups (300g) self-raising flour
¼ cup (60ml) milk

glace icing
2 cups (320g) icing sugar
20g butter, melted
2 tablespoons hot water, approximately

1 Preheat oven to 180°C/160°C fan-forced. Line a 12-hole (⅓-cup/80ml) muffin pan with paper cases.
2 Place ingredients in medium bowl; beat with electric mixer on low speed until ingredients are combined. Increase speed to medium; beat about 3 minutes or until mixture is smooth and paler in colour.
3 Divide mixture among paper cases. Bake about 25 minutes. Stand cakes 5 minutes before turning, top-side up, onto wire racks to cool.
4 Meanwhile, make glace icing. Spread cool cakes with icing.
glace icing Sift icing sugar into small bowl; stir in butter and enough of the water to make a firm paste. Stir over small saucepan of simmering water until icing is spreadable.
preparation time *20 minutes*
cooking time *25 minutes* makes *12*
nutritional count per cake *11.7g total fat (7.1g saturated fat); 1505kJ (360 cal); 58.3g carbohydrate; 4.4g protein; 1g fibre*

cake variations
berry & orange Stir in 1 teaspoon finely grated orange rind and ½ cup dried mixed berries at the end of step 2.
citrus Stir in ½ teaspoon each of finely grated lime, orange and lemon rind at the end of step 2.
passionfruit & white chocolate Stir in ¼ cup passionfruit pulp and ½ cup white Choc Bits at the end of step 2.

icing variations
coconut & lime Stir in ½ teaspoon coconut essence and 1 teaspoon finely grated lime rind.
orange Stir in 1 teaspoon finely grated orange rind. Replace 1 tablespoon of the hot water with orange juice.
passionfruit Stir in 1 tablespoon passionfruit pulp.

caramelised apple tea cakes

mango and coconut jelly cakes

CARAMELISED APPLE TEA CAKES

125g butter, softened
1 teaspoon vanilla extract
⅔ cup (150g) caster sugar
2 eggs
1¼ cups (185g) self-raising flour
½ cup (75g) plain flour
1 teaspoon mixed spice
½ teaspoon ground cinnamon
1 cup (250ml) buttermilk
1 large apple (200g), peeled, grated coarsely

caramelised apples
2 small apples (260g)
75g butter
⅓ cup (75g) firmly packed brown sugar

1 Make caramelised apples.
2 Preheat oven to 180°C/160°C fan-forced. Grease two six-hole (¾-cup/180ml) texas muffin pans with a little butter.
3 Place one slice caramelised apple in each pan hole; spoon caramel sauce over apple.
4 Beat butter, extract and sugar in small bowl with electric mixer until light and fluffy. Beat in eggs, one at a time. Transfer to large bowl; stir in sifted dry ingredients and buttermilk, in two batches. Stir in apple. Divide mixture among pan holes; bake about 30 minutes.
5 Stand cakes 5 minutes before turning, top-side up, onto wire rack. Serve cakes warm.
caramelised apples Slice each unpeeled apple into six 1cm-thick slices. Stir butter and sugar in large frying pan over low heat until sugar dissolves. Add apple slices to caramel sauce; cook, turning occasionally, about 3 minutes or until browned lightly.
preparation time *25 minutes*
cooking time *35 minutes* makes *12*
nutritional count per cake *10.1g total fat (6.2g saturated fat); 974kJ (233 cal); 30.5g carbohydrate; 4.3g protein; 1.1g fibre*

MANGO AND COCONUT JELLY CAKES

2 eggs
⅓ cup (75g) caster sugar
½ cup (75g) self-raising flour
2 teaspoons cornflour
10g butter
2 tablespoons boiling water
1 small mango (300g)
85g packet mango jelly crystals
1¼ cups (310ml) boiling water, extra
1½ cups (115g) shredded coconut
300ml thickened cream

1 Preheat oven to 180°C/160°C fan-forced. Grease 12-hole (½-cup/125ml) oval friand pan with a little butter.
2 Beat eggs in small bowl with electric mixer about 10 minutes or until thick and creamy; gradually add sugar, beating until dissolved between additions. Fold in sifted flours then combined butter and the boiling water.
3 Divide mixture among pan holes. Bake about 12 minutes. Turn cakes immediately onto baking-paper-covered wire rack to cool.
4 Meanwhile, process half the mango until smooth (you need approximately ⅓ cup pulp). Combine jelly and the extra boiling water in large jug, stirring, until jelly dissolves; stir in mango pulp. Strain jelly into shallow dish; refrigerate until jelly is set to the consistency of unbeaten egg white.
5 Dip each cake into jelly then toss in coconut. Refrigerate 30 minutes.
6 Meanwhile, beat cream in small bowl with electric mixer until firm peaks form. Chop remaining mango finely; fold into cream. Cut cakes in half; sandwich with cream.
preparation time *30 minutes (plus refrigeration time)*
cooking time *15 minutes* makes *12*
nutritional count per cake *17.2g total fat (12.4g saturated fat); 1070kJ (256 cal); 21.1g carbohydrate; 3.5g protein; 1.9g fibre*

variation
raspberry and coconut jelly cakes Omit mango jelly and replace with raspberry jelly. Omit fresh mango and replace with 300g fresh raspberries. Process half the berries until smooth, strain; discard seeds. Stir raspberry puree into jelly. Stir remaining raspberries into whipped cream.

HUMMINGBIRD CAKES WITH COCONUT CRUST

440g can crushed pineapple in syrup
1 cup (150g) plain flour
½ cup (75g) self-raising flour
½ teaspoon bicarbonate of soda
½ teaspoon ground cinnamon
½ teaspoon ground ginger
1 cup (220g) firmly packed brown sugar
½ cup (40g) desiccated coconut
1 cup mashed banana
2 eggs, beaten lightly
¾ cup (180ml) vegetable oil

coconut crust
3 cups (225g) shredded coconut
½ cup (110g) firmly packed brown sugar
3 eggs, beaten lightly

1   Preheat oven to 180°C/160°C fan-forced. Line three six-hole (⅓-cup/80ml) muffin pans with paper cases.
2   Drain pineapple over medium bowl, pressing with spoon to extract as much syrup as possible. Reserve ¼ cup of the syrup.
3   Sift flours, soda, spices and sugar into large bowl. Stir in drained pineapple, reserved syrup, coconut, banana, egg and oil. Divide mixture among paper cases. Bake 10 minutes.
4   Meanwhile, make coconut crust by combining ingredients in medium bowl. Spoon crust over cakes; return to oven, bake about 15 minutes.
5   Stand cakes 5 minutes before turning, top-side up, onto wire rack to cool. Serve lightly dusted with sifted icing sugar.
preparation time *25 minutes*
cooking time *25 minutes* makes *18*
nutritional count per cake *10.8g total fat*
(2.5g saturated fat); 874kJ (209 cal);
24.8g carbohydrate; 2.5g protein; 1.3g fibre

tip   You need two large (460g) overripe bananas to get the required amount of mashed banana.

GINGER POWDER PUFFS WITH ORANGE CREAM

2 eggs
⅓ cup (75g) caster sugar
2 tablespoons cornflour
1 tablespoon plain flour
2 tablespoons self-raising flour
1 teaspoon cocoa powder
1½ teaspoons ground ginger
¼ teaspoon ground cinnamon

orange cream
⅔ cup (160ml) thickened cream
2 tablespoons icing sugar
1 teaspoon finely grated orange rind

1   Preheat oven to 180°C/160°C fan-forced. Grease and flour two 12-hole (1½ tablespoon/30ml) shallow round-based patty pans.
2   Beat eggs and sugar in small bowl with electric mixer until thick and creamy. Fold in triple-sifted dry ingredients. Divide mixture among pan holes. Bake about 8 minutes.
3   Working quickly, loosen edges of cakes using palette knife, then turn immediately onto baking-paper-lined wire racks to cool.
4   Meanwhile, make orange cream by beating cream and sifted icing sugar in small bowl with electric mixer until firm peaks form; fold in rind.
5   Just before serving, sandwich puffs together with orange cream. Serve lightly dusted with sifted icing sugar.
serving ideas   Accompany with extra orange cream.
preparation time *25 minutes*
cooking time *10 minutes* makes *12*
nutritional count per puff *5.9g total fat*
(3.5g saturated fat); 451kJ (108 cal);
12.1g carbohydrate; 1.7g protein; 0.1g fibre

hummingbird cakes with coconut crust

ginger powder puffs with orange cream

MARBLED CHOCOLATE MUD CAKES

dark mud cake
85g butter, chopped coarsely
75g dark eating chocolate, chopped coarsely
⅔ cup (150g) caster sugar
½ cup (125ml) milk
½ cup (75g) plain flour
¼ cup (35g) self-raising flour
1 tablespoon cocoa powder
1 egg

white mud cake
85g butter, chopped coarsely
75g white eating chocolate, chopped coarsely
½ cup (110g) caster sugar
⅓ cup (80ml) milk
⅔ cup (100g) plain flour
¼ cup (35g) self-raising flour
1 egg

dark chocolate ganache
⅓ cup (80ml) cream
200g dark eating chocolate, chopped coarsely

white chocolate ganache
2 tablespoons cream
100g white eating chocolate, chopped coarsely

1 Preheat oven to 160°C/140°C fan-forced. Grease two six-hole (¾-cup/180ml) texas muffin pans.
2 Make dark mud cake by combining butter, chocolate, sugar and milk in medium saucepan; stir over low heat until smooth. Transfer to medium bowl; cool 10 minutes. Whisk in sifted flours and cocoa, then egg.
3 Make white mud cake by combining butter, chocolate, sugar and milk in medium saucepan; stir over low heat until smooth. Transfer to medium bowl; cool 10 minutes. Whisk in sifted flours, then egg.
4 Drop alternate spoonfuls of mixtures into pan holes. Pull skewer back and forth through cake mixture several times for a marbled effect. Bake about 30 minutes.
5 Meanwhile, make dark chocolate and white chocolate ganaches.
6 Stand cakes 5 minutes before turning, top-side up, onto wire rack to cool.
7 Spread cakes with dark chocolate ganache; dollop cakes with spoonfuls of white chocolate ganache. Using palette knife, swirl back and forth through ganache for marbled effect.
dark chocolate ganache Stir cream and chocolate in small saucepan over low heat until smooth. Cool 15 minutes.
white chocolate ganache Stir cream and chocolate in small saucepan over low heat until smooth. Cool 15 minutes.
preparation time *30 minutes (plus cooling time)*
cooking time *40 minutes* makes *12*
nutritional count per cake *17.3g total fat (10.8g saturated fat); 1488kJ (356 cal); 44.7g carbohydrate; 4.8g protein; 0.9g fibre*

FRIANDS

MANDARIN AND POPPY SEED FRIANDS

2 large mandarins (500g)
1 tablespoon poppy seeds
2 tablespoons mandarin juice
6 egg whites
185g butter, melted
1 cup (120g) almond meal
1½ cups (240g) icing sugar
½ cup (75g) plain flour

1 Preheat oven to 200°C/180°C fan-forced. Line 12-hole
(½-cup/125ml) oval friand pan with paper cases.
2 Finely grate rind from mandarins (you need 2 tablespoons of
rind). Juice the mandarins (you need 2 tablespoons of juice).
3 Combine poppy seeds and juice in small jug; stand 10 minutes.
4 Place egg whites in medium bowl; whisk lightly with fork until
combined. Add butter, almond meal, sifted icing sugar and flour,
rind and poppy seed mixture; stir until combined.
5 Divide mixture among pan holes. Bake about 20 minutes. Stand
friands 5 minutes before turning, top-side up, onto wire rack to cool.
Serve lightly dusted with sifted icing sugar.
preparation time *15 minutes*
cooking time *20 minutes* makes *12*
nutritional count per friand *18.7g total fat (8.7g saturated fat);*
1262kJ (302 cal); 27.7g carbohydrate; 5g protein; 2g fibre

tip Store friands in an airtight container for up to three days.

variation
lemon poppy seed friands Omit the mandarin juice and replace
with 2 tablespoons lemon juice. Omit the mandarin rind and
replace with 1 tablespoon finely grated lemon rind.

COFFEE AND WALNUT FRIANDS

1¼ cups (125g) roasted walnuts
2 teaspoons instant coffee granules
2 teaspoons boiling water
6 egg whites
185g butter, melted
1½ cups (240g) icing sugar
½ cup (75g) plain flour
24 whole coffee beans

1 Preheat oven to 200°C/180°C fan-forced. Grease 12-hole (½-cup/125ml) oval friand pan.
2 Process nuts until ground finely.
3 Stir coffee and the water in small jug until dissolved.
4 Place egg whites in medium bowl; whisk lightly with fork until combined. Add butter, sifted icing sugar and flour, nuts and coffee mixture; stir until combined.
5 Divide mixture among pans; top each friand with two coffee beans. Bake about 20 minutes. Stand friands 5 minutes before turning, top-side up, onto wire rack to cool. Serve lightly dusted with sifted icing sugar.

preparation time *15 minutes*
cooking time *20 minutes* makes *12*
nutritional count per friand *19.9g total fat (8.8g saturated fat); 1237kJ (296 cal); 24.9g carbohydrate; 4.1g protein; 0.9g fibre*

tip Store friands in an airtight container for up to three days.

variation

hazelnut and coffee friands Omit the walnuts and replace with 125g hazelnut meal.

LEMON AND CRANBERRY FRIANDS

6 egg whites
185g butter, melted
1 cup (120g) almond meal
1½ cups (240g) icing sugar
½ cup (75g) plain flour
¾ cup (105g) dried cranberries
1 tablespoon finely grated lemon rind
1 tablespoon lemon juice

1 Preheat oven to 200°C/180°C fan-forced. Grease 12-hole (½-cup/125ml) oval friand pan.
2 Place egg whites in medium bowl; whisk lightly with fork until combined. Add butter, almond meal, sifted icing sugar and flour, berries, rind and juice; stir until combined.
3 Divide mixture among pan holes. Bake about 20 minutes. Stand friands 5 minutes before turning, top-side up, onto wire rack to cool. Serve lightly dusted with sifted icing sugar.

preparation time *15 minutes*
cooking time *20 minutes* makes *12*
nutritional count per friand *18.3g total fat (8.7g saturated fat); 1304kJ (312 cal); 31.3g carbohydrate; 4.8g protein; 1.6g fibre*

tip Store friands in an airtight container for up to three days.

variation

orange and blueberry friands Omit dried cranberries and replace with ¾ cup (105g) dried blueberries. Omit lemon rind and replace with 1½ tablespoons finely grated orange rind. Omit lemon juice and replace with 1 tablespoon orange juice.

coffee and walnut friands

lemon and cranberry friands

choc-hazelnut friands

brandied cherry friands

CHOC-HAZELNUT FRIANDS

6 egg whites
185g butter, melted
1 cup (100g) hazelnut meal
1½ cups (240g) icing sugar
½ cup (75g) plain flour
1 tablespoon cocoa powder
100g dark eating chocolate, chopped finely
¼ cup (35g) coarsely chopped, roasted hazelnuts

1 Preheat oven to 200°C/180°C fan-forced. Line 12-hole (½-cup/125ml) oval friand pan with paper cases.
2 Place egg whites in medium bowl; whisk lightly with fork until combined. Add butter, hazelnut meal, sifted icing sugar, flour and cocoa, and chocolate; stir until combined.
3 Divide mixture among pan holes; sprinkle with nuts. Bake about 25 minutes. Stand friands 5 minutes before turning, top-side up, onto wire rack to cool.
preparation time *15 minutes*
cooking time *25 minutes* makes *12*
nutritional count per friand *23.4g total fat (10.2g saturated fat); 1488kJ (356 cal); 30.7g carbohydrate; 5.2g protein; 1.8g fibre*

tips Store friands in an airtight container for up to three days.
We used freeform paper cases made by pushing a 12cm square of paper (we used paper about the same thickness as printer paper) into ungreased pan holes, followed by a 12cm square of baking paper.

variation

choc-pecan friands Omit hazelnut meal and replace with 100g finely ground pecans. Omit hazelnuts and replace with 35g coarsely chopped pecans.

BRANDIED CHERRY FRIANDS

1 cup (150g) frozen seeded cherries
2 tablespoons brandy
1 cup (120g) roasted pecans
6 egg whites
185g butter, melted
1½ cups (240g) icing sugar
½ cup (75g) plain flour

cherry sauce
¼ cup (55g) caster sugar
2 tablespoons water

1 Preheat oven to 200°C/180°C fan-forced. Grease 12-hole (½-cup/125ml) oval friand pan.
2 Combine cherries and brandy in small bowl; stand 30 minutes. Drain cherries; reserve liquid.
3 Process nuts until ground finely.
4 Place egg whites in medium bowl; whisk lightly with fork until combined. Add butter, sifted icing sugar and flour, and nuts. Divide mixture among pan holes; top with drained cherries. Bake about 20 minutes.
5 Meanwhile, make cherry sauce.
6 Stand friands 5 minutes before turning, top-side up, onto serving plates. Serve with cherry sauce.
cherry sauce Combine sugar, the water and reserved cherry juice in small saucepan; stir over low heat until sugar dissolves. Bring to the boil; reduce heat. Simmer, uncovered, about 3 minutes or until sauce thickens slightly.
preparation time *15 minutes (plus standing time)*
cooking time *20 minutes* makes *12*
nutritional count per friand *19.9g total fat (8.8g saturated fat); 1363kJ (326 cal); 31g carbohydrate; 3.7g protein; 1.3g fibre*

COCONUT AND PINEAPPLE FRIANDS

6 egg whites
185g butter, melted
1 cup (120g) almond meal
1½ cups (240g) icing sugar
⅓ cup (50g) plain flour
¾ cup (170g) finely chopped glacé pineapple
½ cup (40g) shredded coconut

1 Preheat oven to 200°C/180°C fan-forced. Line 12-hole (½-cup/125ml) oval friand pan with paper cases.
2 Place egg whites in medium bowl; whisk lightly with fork until combined. Add butter, almond meal, sifted icing sugar and flour, pineapple and ⅓ cup of the coconut; stir until combined. Divide mixture among pan holes; sprinkle with remaining coconut. Bake about 20 minutes.
3 Stand friands 5 minutes before turning, top-side up, onto wire rack to cool.
preparation time *15 minutes*
cooking time *20 minutes* makes *12*
nutritional count per friand *20.4g total fat (10.6g saturated fat); 1404kJ (336 cal); 33.1g carbohydrate; 4.6g protein; 1.6g fibre*

tips Store friands in an airtight container for up to three days.
We used freeform paper cases made by pushing a 12cm square of paper (we used paper about the same thickness as printer paper) into ungreased pan holes, followed by a 12cm square of baking paper.

variation
peach and coconut friands Omit the glacé pineapple and replace with 150g finely chopped glacé peach.

PISTACHIO AND LIME FRIANDS

1 cup (140g) unsalted roasted pistachios
6 egg whites
185g butter, melted
1½ cups (240g) icing sugar
½ cup (75g) plain flour
2 teaspoons finely grated lime rind
1 tablespoon lime juice

1 Preheat oven to 200°C/180°C fan-forced. Line 12-hole (½-cup/125ml) oval friand pan.
2 Process nuts until ground finely.
3 Place egg whites in medium bowl; whisk lightly with fork until combined. Add butter, sifted icing sugar and flour, rind, juice and nuts; stir until combined. Divide mixture among pan holes. Bake about 25 minutes.
4 Stand friands 5 minutes before turning, top-side up, onto wire rack to cool. Serve dusted with a little sifted icing sugar.
preparation time *15 minutes*
cooking time *25 minutes* makes *12*
nutritional count per friand *18.6g total fat (9g saturated fat); 1229kJ (294 cal); 26.4g carbohydrate; 4.9g protein; 1.3g fibre*

tips Store friands in an airtight container for up to three days.
We used freeform paper cases made by pushing a 12cm square of paper (we used paper about the same thickness as printer paper) into ungreased pan holes, followed by a 12cm square of baking paper.

coconut and pineapple friands

pistachio and lime friands

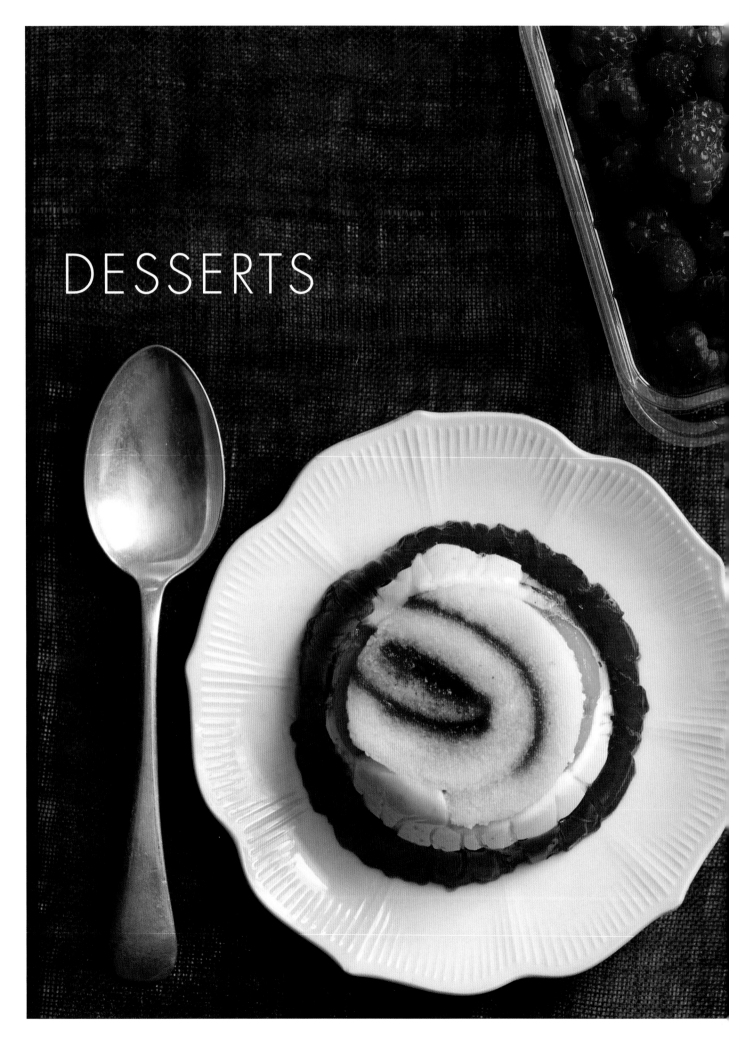

DESSERTS

WHITE CHOCOLATE
AND RASPBERRY TRIFLES

½ jam-filled sponge roll (200g)
¼ cup (60ml) sweet sherry
400g can peach halves in natural juice, drained
2 tablespoons custard powder
2 tablespoons caster sugar
½ cup (125ml) cream
½ cup (125ml) milk
1 vanilla bean
125g white eating chocolate, chopped coarsely
85g packet raspberry jelly crystals
1 cup (150g) frozen raspberries

1 Line each hole of a six-hole (¾-cup/180ml) texas muffin pan
with plastic wrap. Cut sponge roll into six 1.5cm-thick slices; cut
6.5cm rounds from each slice, discard remainder. Place one round
in each pan hole; brush with sherry. Place one peach half, cut-side
down, in each pan hole; gently press peaches to flatten slightly.
2 Combine custard powder and sugar in small saucepan; gradually
stir in cream and milk. Split vanilla bean in half lengthways; scrape
seeds into pan (reserve pod for another use). Cook, stirring, until mixture
boils and thickens. Remove from heat; stir in chocolate until smooth.
3 Pour custard into pan holes; smooth surface. Refrigerate 30 minutes.
4 Meanwhile, make jelly according to manufacturer's instructions;
refrigerate until jelly is set to the consistency of unbeaten egg white.
5 Sprinkle berries over custard; spoon jelly over berries; refrigerate
3 hours or overnight.
6 Turn onto serving plates, top side-down, gently remove plastic wrap.
serving idea Serve accompanied by fresh raspberries.
preparation time *30 minutes (plus refrigeration time)*
cooking time *5 minutes* makes 6
nutritional count per trifle *19.2g total fat (12g saturated fat);
1914kJ (458 cal); 61.6g carbohydrate; 5.8g protein; 2.4g fibre*

TIRAMISU

460g double unfilled round sponge cake
2 tablespoons instant coffee granules
¼ cup (60ml) boiling water
⅓ cup (80ml) coffee-flavoured liqueur
1 teaspoon gelatine
1 tablespoon boiling water, extra
¾ cup (180ml) thickened cream
¼ cup (40g) icing sugar
1 teaspoon vanilla extract
1½ cups (375g) mascarpone cheese

ganache
⅔ cup (160ml) cream
180g dark eating chocolate, chopped coarsely

1 Make ganache.
2 Line each hole of a greased six-hole (¾-cup/180ml) texas muffin pan with plastic wrap. Divide half the ganache over the base of each pan hole. Refrigerate 20 minutes.
3 Meanwhile, cut each sponge cake into three slices horizontally. Cut six 8cm rounds from three sponge slices and six 7cm rounds from remaining three sponge slices.
4 Dissolve coffee in the boiling water in small jug; stir in liqueur.
5 Sprinkle gelatine over the extra boiling water in another small jug; stir until gelatine dissolves. Cool.
6 Beat cream, sifted icing sugar and extract in small bowl with electric mixer until soft peaks form; beat in gelatine mixture. Transfer mixture to large bowl; fold in cheese.
7 Brush both sides of sponge rounds with coffee mixture. Spread half the cheese mixture into the pan holes; top with small sponge rounds. Spread remaining cheese mixture over sponge layers; top with larger sponge rounds.
8 Spread remaining ganache over sponge layers; refrigerate 3 hours or overnight.
9 Remove tiramisu from pan; turn, top-side down, onto serving plates, remove plastic wrap. Serve dusted with a little sifted cocoa powder.
ganache Bring cream to the boil in small saucepan; remove from heat. Add chocolate; stir until smooth.
serving ideas Serve accompanied by fresh blueberries.
preparation time *35 minutes (plus refrigeration time)*
cooking time *5 minutes* makes *6*
nutritional count per tiramisu *70.5g total fat (44.6g saturated fat); 4255kJ (1018 cal); 80.6g carbohydrate; 10.8g protein; 2.1g fibre*

tip Stand remaining ganache at room temperature so it is a spreadable consistency when topping tiramisu.

BLOOD ORANGE MERINGUE PIES

½ cup (110g) caster sugar
2 tablespoons cornflour
⅔ cup (160ml) blood orange juice
2 tablespoons water
2 teaspoons finely grated blood orange rind
75g unsalted butter, chopped coarsely
2 eggs, separated
½ cup (110g) caster sugar, extra

pastry
1¼ cups (185g) plain flour
¼ cup (55g) caster sugar
125g cold butter, chopped coarsely
1 egg yolk

1 Make pastry.
2 Grease 12-hole (⅓-cup/80ml) muffin pan. Roll pastry between sheets of baking paper to 4mm thickness; cut out twelve 8cm rounds. Press rounds into pan holes; prick bases all over with fork. Refrigerate 30 minutes.
3 Preheat oven to 200°C/180°C fan-forced.
4 Bake pastry cases 10 minutes. Cool.
5 Meanwhile, combine sugar and cornflour in small saucepan; gradually stir in juice and the water until smooth. Cook, stirring, until mixture boils and thickens. Reduce heat; simmer, stirring, 1 minute. Remove from heat; stir in rind, butter and egg yolks. Cool 10 minutes.
6 Divide filling among pastry cases. Refrigerate 1 hour.
7 Increase temperature to 240°C/220°C fan-forced.
8 Beat egg whites in small bowl with electric mixer until soft peaks form; gradually add extra sugar, beating until sugar dissolves.
9 Roughen surface of filling with fork; using star nozzle, pipe meringue over filling. Bake about 3 minutes or until browned lightly.

pastry Process flour, sugar and butter until coarse. Add egg yolk; process until combined. Knead on lightly floured surface until smooth. Cover; refrigerate 30 minutes.

preparation time *30 minutes*
(plus refrigeration and cooling time)
cooking time *20 minutes* makes *12*
nutritional count per pie *15.3g total fat*
(9.5g saturated fat); 1250kJ (299 cal);
36.7 carbohydrate; 3.2g protein; 0.6g fibre

tip If pastry is too dry, add 2 teaspoons of water with the egg yolk.

variation
lemon meringue tarts Increase the sugar in filling to ⅔ cup. Omit orange rind and replace with 2 teaspoons finely grated lemon rind. Omit orange juice and replace with ⅔ cup lemon juice.

BAKLAVA FIGS

6 sheets fillo pastry
50g butter, melted
12 large fresh figs (960g)
⅓ cup (75g) firmly packed brown sugar
1 teaspoon mixed spice
½ teaspoon ground cinnamon
80g butter, chopped coarsely
½ cup (60g) finely chopped roasted walnuts
¼ cup (35g) slivered almonds
1 teaspoon finely grated orange rind

maple cream
300ml thickened cream
2 tablespoons maple syrup

1 Preheat oven to 200°C/180°C fan-forced. Grease 12-hole (⅓-cup/80ml) muffin pan.
2 Brush three pastry sheets with melted butter; stack together. Repeat with remaining pastry. Cut each pastry stack into six rectangles (you will have 12 rectangles). Gently press one stack into each pan hole.
3 Quarter each fig, cutting three-quarters of the way down the fig. Place one fig in each pastry case.
4 Combine sugar and spices in medium bowl; using fingers, rub in chopped butter. Stir in nuts and rind; gently push mixture into the centre of figs. Bake about 15 minutes.
5 Meanwhile, make maple cream.
6 Serve baklava figs, dusted with a little sifted icing sugar, and maple cream.
maple cream Beat cream and syrup in small bowl with electric mixer until soft peaks form.
preparation time *20 minutes*
cooking time *15 minutes* makes *12*
nutritional count per baklava *23.7g total fat (12.3g saturated fat); 1308kJ (313 cal); 20.5g carbohydrate; 3.7g protein; 2.7g fibre*

WHITE CHOCOLATE AND RASPBERRY BREAD PUDDINGS

3 small croissants (150g)
100g white eating chocolate, chopped coarsely
1 cup (150g) fresh raspberries
1¼ cups (310ml) milk
¾ cup (180ml) cream
2 tablespoons caster sugar
½ teaspoon vanilla extract
3 eggs

1 Preheat oven to 160°C/140°C fan-forced. Grease six-hole (¾-cup/180ml) texas muffin pan; line each pan hole with two criss-crossed 5cm x 20cm strips of baking paper.
2 Split each croissant in half lengthways then tear each half into pieces. Roughly line each pan hole with croissant pieces. Sprinkle with chocolate and berries.
3 Combine milk, cream, sugar and extract in small saucepan; bring to the boil. Whisk eggs in large bowl; gradually whisk in hot milk mixture. Pour custard into pan holes.
4 Place pan in large baking dish; add enough boiling water to come halfway up sides of pan. Bake about 35 minutes or until puddings set. Remove pan from dish; stand puddings 15 minutes. Using baking paper strips, lift puddings from pan holes onto serving plates. Serve dusted with a little sifted icing sugar.
serving idea Serve accompanied by fresh raspberries.
preparation time *20 minutes (plus standing time)*
cooking time *40 minutes* makes *6*
nutritional count per pudding *29.2g total fat (17.4g saturated fat); 1760kJ (421 cal); 29.7g carbohydrate; 9.6g protein; 2.1g fibre*

variation
dark chocolate and fig bread pudding Omit the white chocolate and replace with 100g coarsely chopped dark eating chocolate. Omit the raspberries and replace with 2 coarsely chopped fresh large figs.

baklava figs

white chocolate and raspberry bread puddings

SOFT-CENTRED MOCHA PUDDINGS

150g dark eating chocolate, chopped coarsely
125g butter, chopped coarsely
3 teaspoons instant coffee granules
2 eggs
2 egg yolks
⅓ cup (75g) caster sugar
¼ cup (35g) plain flour
2 teaspoons cocoa powder

1 Preheat oven to 200°C/180°C fan-forced. Grease six-hole (¾-cup/180ml) texas muffin pan well with softened butter.

2 Stir chocolate, butter and coffee in small saucepan, over low heat, until smooth; cool 10 minutes. Transfer to a large bowl.

3 Beat eggs, egg yolks and sugar in small bowl with electric mixer until thick and creamy. Fold egg mixture and sifted flour into barely warm chocolate mixture.

4 Divide mixture among pan holes; bake, in oven, 12 minutes.

5 Gently turn puddings onto serving plates, top-side down. Serve immediately, dusted with sifted cocoa powder.

serving ideas Serve with whipped cream and fresh raspberries.

preparation time *35 minutes*
cooking time *5 minutes* makes *6*
nutritional count per pudding *28.6g total fat (16.7g saturated fat); 1697kJ (406 cal); 32.9g carbohydrate; 5.7g protein; 0.9g fibre*

tip Use a good-quality dark chocolate with 70% cocoa solids.

BERRY AND RHUBARB PIES

2 cups (220g) coarsely chopped rhubarb
¼ cup (55g) caster sugar
2 tablespoons water
1 tablespoon cornflour
2 cups (300g) frozen mixed berries
1 egg white
2 teaspoons caster sugar, extra

pastry
1⅔ cups (250g) plain flour
⅓ cup (75g) caster sugar
150g cold butter, chopped coarsely
1 egg yolk

1   Make pastry.
2   Place rhubarb, sugar and half the water in medium saucepan; bring to the boil. Reduce heat; simmer, covered, about 3 minutes or until rhubarb is tender. Blend cornflour with the remaining water; stir into rhubarb mixture. Stir over heat until mixture boils and thickens. Remove from heat; stir in berries. Cool.
3   Grease six-hole (¾-cup/180ml) texas muffin pan. Roll two-thirds of the pastry between sheets of baking paper to 4mm thickness; cut out six 12cm rounds. Press rounds into pan holes. Refrigerate 30 minutes.
4   Preheat oven to 200°C/180°C fan-forced.
5   Roll remaining pastry between sheets of baking paper to 4mm thickness; cut out six 9cm rounds.
6   Divide fruit mixture among pastry cases.
7   Brush edge of 9cm rounds with egg white; place over filling. Press edges firmly to seal. Brush tops with egg white; sprinkle with extra sugar. Bake about 30 minutes.
8   Stand pies in pan 10 minutes; using palette knife, loosen pies from edge of pan before lifting out. Serve warm.

pastry   Process flour, sugar and butter until coarse. Add egg yolk; process until combined. Knead on floured surface until smooth. Cover; refrigerate 30 minutes.
serving idea   Serve with vanilla ice-cream.
preparation time *30 minutes (plus refrigeration time)*
cooking time *35 minutes* makes 6
nutritional count per pie   *22.1g total fat
(13.9g saturated fat); 1946kJ (464 cal);
57.1g carbohydrate; 7.2g protein; 3.9g fibre*

tips   You need four large stems of rhubarb to get the required amount of chopped rhubarb.
If pastry is too dry, add 2 teaspoons of water with the egg yolk.

variation

apple and blackberry pies   Omit rhubarb and replace with 2 peeled, coarsely chopped medium apples. Cook with sugar and the water for about 5 minutes or until apples are just tender. Omit mixed berries and replace with 150g blackberries.

chocolate, peanut and caramel cheesecakes

caramel cashew tarts

CHOCOLATE, PEANUT AND CARAMEL CHEESECAKES

12 (110g) chocolate ripple biscuits
1 teaspoon gelatine
1 tablespoon water
250g cream cheese, softened
⅓ cup (75g) caster sugar
¾ cup (180ml) cream
2 x 60g Snickers bars, chopped finely
¼ cup (35g) crushed nuts
100g milk eating chocolate, chopped coarsely
2 tablespoons cream, extra

1 Line each hole of a greased six-hole (¾-cup/180ml) texas muffin pan with plastic wrap. Chop biscuits into 1cm pieces; divide among pan holes.
2 Sprinkle gelatine over the water in small heatproof jug. Stand jug in small saucepan of simmering water; stir until gelatine dissolves, cool 5 minutes.
3 Beat cream cheese and sugar in small bowl with electric mixer until smooth; beat in cream until combined. Stir in gelatine mixture, chocolate bar and nuts.
4 Divide mixture among pan holes; smooth surface. Refrigerate overnight.
5 Combine chocolate and extra cream in small saucepan; cook, stirring, over low heat until smooth.
6 Lift cheesecakes from pan, remove plastic wrap; turn, top-side up, onto plates. Drizzle with chocolate sauce.
serving idea Serve with vanilla ice-cream.
preparation time *15 minutes (plus refrigeration time)* cooking time 3 minutes makes 6
nutritional count per cheesecake *46.2g total fat (27.5g saturated fat); 2730kJ (653 cal); 48.9g carbohydrate; 10.2g protein; 2.2g fibre*

CARAMEL CASHEW TARTS

1 cup (150g) roasted unsalted cashews
1 tablespoon cornflour
¾ cup (165g) firmly packed brown sugar
2 tablespoons golden syrup
50g butter, melted
2 eggs
2 tablespoons cream
1 teaspoon vanilla extract

pastry
1¼ cups (185g) plain flour
¼ cup (55g) caster sugar
125g cold butter, chopped coarsely
1 egg yolk
2 teaspoons water

cinnamon cream
300ml thickened cream
1 tablespoon icing sugar
1 teaspoon ground cinnamon

1 Make pastry.
2 Grease two 12-hole (⅓-cup/80ml) muffin pans. Roll pastry between sheets of baking paper to 3mm thickness; cut out twenty-four 8cm rounds. Press rounds into pan holes; prick bases all over with fork. Refrigerate 20 minutes.
3 Preheat oven to 200°C/180°C fan-forced.
4 Bake pastry cases 10 minutes. Cool.
5 Reduce temperature to 160°C/140°C fan-forced.
6 Combine nuts and cornflour in medium bowl; stir in sugar, syrup, butter, egg, cream and extract. Divide filling among pastry cases. Bake about 15 minutes; cool. Refrigerate 30 minutes.
7 Meanwhile, beat ingredients for cinnamon cream in small bowl with electric mixer until soft peaks form.
8 Serve tarts with cinnamon cream.
pastry Process flour, sugar and butter until coarse. Add egg yolk and the water; process until combined. Knead on floured surface until smooth. Cover; refrigerate 30 minutes.
preparation time *20 minutes (plus refrigeration and cooling time)* cooking time *25 minutes* makes *24*
nutritional count per tart *15.2g total fat (8.2g saturated fat); 932kJ (223 cal); 18.6g carbohydrate; 29g protein; 0.7g fibre*

tip If pastry is too dry, add 2 teaspoons of water with the egg yolk.

ORANGE BLOSSOM MERINGUES WITH POMEGRANATE SYRUP

4 egg whites
1 cup (220g) caster sugar
1 teaspoon orange blossom water
300ml thickened cream

pomegranate syrup
2 tablespoons caster sugar
2 tablespoons water
½ cup (125ml) pomegranate pulp

1 Preheat oven to 120°C/100°C fan-forced. Grease six-hole (¾-cup/180ml) texas muffin pan; line each pan hole with two criss-crossed 5cm x 20cm strips of baking paper.

2 Beat egg whites in small bowl with electric mixer until soft peaks form; gradually add sugar, beating until sugar dissolves. Beat in blossom water until combined.

3 Divide meringue among pan holes; use the back of a spoon to create a swirl on top. Bake about 30 minutes. Turn off oven; cool meringues in oven with door ajar.

4 Meanwhile, make pomegranate syrup.

5 Using baking paper strips, remove meringues from pan. Serve, top-side up, with pomegranate syrup.

pomegranate syrup Stir sugar and the water in small saucepan over heat until sugar dissolves; bring to the boil. Boil, uncovered, about 2 minutes or until thickened slightly. Add pulp; simmer 2 minutes. Cool.

serving idea Serve with whipped cream.

preparation time *20 minutes (plus cooling time)*
cooking time *40 minutes* makes 6
nutritional count per meringue *18.6g total fat (12.2g saturated fat); 1563kJ (374 cal); 47.1g carbohydrate; 3.8g protein; 1.3g fibre*

tip You need two medium pomegranates (640g) to get the required amount of pomegranate pulp.

CRÈME BRÛLÉE PRALINE TARTS

1⅓ cups (330ml) cream
⅓ cup (80ml) milk
1 vanilla bean
4 egg yolks
¼ cup (55g) caster sugar

pastry
1¼ cups (185g) plain flour
¼ cup (55g) caster sugar
125g cold butter, chopped coarsely
1 egg yolk

praline
¼ cup (55g) caster sugar
2 tablespoons water
1 tablespoon roasted hazelnuts
2 tablespoons unsalted roasted pistachios

1 Make pastry.
2 Grease six-hole (¾-cup/180ml) texas muffin pan. Cut six 11cm rounds from pastry. Press rounds into pan holes; prick bases all over with fork. Refrigerate 30 minutes.
3 Preheat oven to 160°C/140°C fan-forced.
4 Combine cream and milk in small saucepan. Split vanilla bean in half lengthways; scrape seeds into pan (reserve pod for another use). Bring to the boil. Beat egg yolks and sugar in small bowl with electric mixer until thick and creamy. Gradually whisk hot cream mixture into egg mixture. Pour warm custard into pastry cases.
5 Bake about 30 minutes or until set; cool 15 minutes. Refrigerate 1 hour.
6 Meanwhile, make praline.
7 Preheat grill. Remove tarts from pan; place on oven tray. Sprinkle custard with praline; grill until praline caramelises. Serve immediately.

pastry Process flour, sugar and butter until coarse. Add egg yolk; process until combined. Knead on floured surface until smooth. Roll pastry between sheets of baking paper to 4mm thickness. Refrigerate 15 minutes.

praline Combine sugar and the water in small saucepan; stir over heat until sugar dissolves. Boil, uncovered, without stirring, about 8 minutes or until golden in colour. Place nuts, in single layer, on greased oven tray. Pour toffee over nuts; stand about 15 minutes or until set. Break toffee into large pieces; process until chopped finely.

preparation time *35 minutes*
(plus refrigeration, standing and cooling time)
cooking time *40 minutes* makes *6*
nutritional count per tart *49.8g total fat (29.1g saturated fat); 2901kJ (694 cal); 52.8g carbohydrate; 8.7g protein; 1.8g fibre*

tip If pastry is too dry, add 2 teaspoons of water with egg yolk.

DARK CHOCOLATE AND HAZELNUT FROZEN PARFAIT

½ cup (125ml) thickened cream
½ cup (165g) chocolate-hazelnut spread
¼ cup (60ml) coffee-flavoured liqueur
2 eggs
3 egg yolks
⅓ cup (75g) caster sugar
1 cup (250ml) thickened cream, extra
140g dark eating chocolate, grated coarsely
⅓ cup (40g) finely chopped roasted hazelnuts
100g dark eating chocolate, grated coarsely, extra

1 Line six-hole (¾-cup/180ml) texas muffin pan with paper cases.
2 Combine cream, chocolate-hazelnut spread and liqueur in small saucepan; stir over low heat until smooth.
3 Beat eggs, egg yolks and sugar in small bowl with electric mixer until thick and creamy; with motor operating, gradually beat warm chocolate mixture into egg mixture. Transfer parfait to large bowl; refrigerate 20 minutes or until mixture thickens slightly.
4 Beat extra cream in small bowl with electric mixer until soft peaks form; fold into parfait with grated chocolate and nuts. Pour mixture into cases. Cover loosely with plastic wrap; freeze overnight.
5 Lift parfaits out of pan; serve immediately, topped with extra grated chocolate.
preparation time *20 minutes*
(plus refrigeration and freezing time)
cooking time *10 minutes* makes *6*
nutritional count per parfait *52.4g total fat*
(26.4g saturated fat); 3231kJ (773 cal);
61.2g carbohydrate; 9.9g protein; 1.5g fibre

tip We used freeform paper cases made by pushing a 16cm square of paper (we used paper about the same thickness as printer paper) into ungreased pan holes, followed by a 16cm square of baking paper.

variation

white chocolate and macadamia frozen parfaits Omit chocolate-hazelnut spread and replace with 150g melted white eating chocolate. Omit grated dark chocolate. Omit hazelnuts and replace with ⅓ cup finely chopped roasted macadamias. Top parfaits with 100g coarsely grated white eating chocolate.

STICKY BANANA PUDDINGS WITH BUTTERSCOTCH SAUCE

125g butter, softened
⅔ cup (150g) firmly packed brown sugar
2 eggs
1½ cups (225g) self-raising flour
1 teaspoon mixed spice
1 cup mashed banana
¼ cup (60g) sour cream
¼ cup (60ml) milk
2 tablespoons brown sugar, extra
1 large banana (230g), sliced thinly

butterscotch sauce
½ cup (110g) firmly packed brown sugar
⅔ cup (160ml) cream
50g butter

1 Preheat oven to 180°C/160°C fan-forced. Grease eight holes of two six-hole (¾-cup/180ml) texas muffin pans.
2 Beat butter and sugar in small bowl with electric mixer until light and fluffy. Beat in eggs, one at a time; transfer mixture to large bowl. Stir in sifted flour and spice, mashed banana, sour cream and milk in two batches.
3 Sprinkle extra sugar in pan holes; cover bases of pan holes with sliced banana. Divide cake mixture among pan holes. Bake 30 minutes.
4 Meanwhile, make butterscotch sauce.
5 Turn puddings, top-side down, onto serving plates; serve warm with butterscotch sauce.
butterscotch sauce Combine ingredients in small saucepan; stir over heat, without boiling, until sugar dissolves. Simmer, stirring, about 3 minutes or until sauce thickens slightly.
serving idea Serve with vanilla ice-cream.
preparation time *15 minutes*
cooking time *30 minutes* makes *8*
nutritional count per pudding *31.6g total fat*
(20.1g saturated fat); 2404kJ (575 cal);
65.5g carbohydrate; 6.3g protein; 2.1g fibre

tip You need 2 large (460g) overripe bananas to get the required amount of mashed banana.

dark chocolate and hazelnut frozen parfait   sticky banana puddings with butterscotch sauce

AFTER-DINNER TREATS

PORTUGUESE CUSTARD TARTS

½ cup (110g) caster sugar
2 tablespoons cornflour
3 egg yolks
¾ cup (180ml) milk
½ cup (125ml) cream
1 vanilla bean, split lengthways
5cm strip lemon rind
1 sheet ready-rolled butter puff pastry

1 Preheat oven to 220°C/200°C fan-forced. Grease
two 12-hole (1-tablespoon/20ml) mini muffin pans.
2 Combine sugar and cornflour in medium saucepan.
Gradually whisk in combined egg yolks, milk and cream.
3 Scrape vanilla bean seeds into custard; add rind.
Stir over medium heat until mixture just comes to the
boil. Remove from heat; discard rind. Cover surface of
custard with plastic wrap while making pastry cases.
4 Cut pastry sheet in half; place two halves on top
of each other. Roll pastry up tightly from long side; cut
log into 24 rounds.
5 Roll each pastry round on floured surface to
6cm diameter. Press pastry into pan holes.
6 Divide custard among pastry cases. Bake about
12 minutes. Turn, top-side up, onto wire rack to cool.
Serve dusted with a little sifted icing sugar.
preparation time *25 minutes (plus cooling time)*
cooking time *20 minutes* makes *24*
nutritional count per tart *4.8g total fat*
(2.7g saturated fat); 339kJ (81 cal);
8.3g carbohydrate; 1.1g protein; 0.1g fibre

CARAMEL TARTS

18 (220g) butternut snap biscuits
395g can sweetened condensed milk
60g butter, chopped coarsely
⅓ cup (75g) firmly packed brown sugar
1 tablespoon lemon juice

1 Preheat oven to 160°C/140°C fan-forced. Grease two 12-hole (1½-tablespoons/30ml) shallow round-based patty pans.
2 Place one biscuit each over top of 18 pan holes. Bake about 4 minutes or until biscuits soften. Using the back of a teaspoon, gently press softened biscuits into pan holes; cool.
3 Combine condensed milk, butter and sugar in small heavy-based saucepan; stir over heat until smooth. Bring to the boil; boil, stirring, about 10 minutes or until mixture is thick and dark caramel in colour. Remove from heat; stir in juice.
4 Divide mixture among biscuit cases; refrigerate 30 minutes or until set.

preparation time *25 minutes (plus refrigeration time)*
cooking time *10 minutes* makes *18*
nutritional count per tart *7.7g total fat*
(5g saturated fat); 727kJ (174 cal);
23.2g carbohydrate; 2.6g protein; 0.4g fibre

orange caramels

passionfruit marshmallows

ORANGE CARAMELS

1 cup (220g) caster sugar
90g unsalted butter
2 tablespoons golden syrup
⅓ cup (115g) glucose syrup
½ cup (125ml) sweetened condensed milk
¼ cup (60ml) cream
2 teaspoons finely grated orange rind
¼ cup (30g) finely chopped unsalted, roasted pistachios

1 Grease two 12-hole (1-tablespoon/20ml) mini muffin pans.
2 Combine sugar, butter, syrups, condensed milk and cream in medium heavy-based saucepan; stir over heat, without boiling, until sugar dissolves. Bring to the boil; boil, stirring, about 8 minutes or until mixture is caramel in colour. Stir in rind. Remove pan from heat; allow bubbles to subside.
3 Divide mixture among pan holes; sprinkle with nuts. Stand 20 minutes before removing from pan with greased palette knife.

preparation time *15 minutes (plus standing time)*
cooking time *10 minutes* makes *24*
nutritional count per serving *5.5g total fat (3.3g saturated fat); 535kJ (128 cal); 18.6g carbohydrate; 0.9g protein; 0.1g fibre*

PASSIONFRUIT MARSHMALLOWS

2 cups (160g) desiccated coconut
⅓ cup (80ml) passionfruit pulp
1 tablespoon (14g) gelatine
¼ cup (60ml) cold water
1 cup (220g) caster sugar
½ cup (125ml) hot water

1 Grease two 12-hole (1-tablespoon/20ml) mini muffin pans. Sprinkle inside of pan holes with a little of the coconut; shake pan to coat base and side of holes.
2 Strain passionfruit into small bowl; discard seeds.
3 Sprinkle gelatine over the cold water in small bowl.
4 Stir passionfruit juice, sugar and the hot water in small heavy-based saucepan over heat until sugar dissolves; bring to the boil. Stir in gelatine mixture; boil, without stirring, 15 minutes. Transfer to small bowl of electric mixer; cool to lukewarm.
5 Beat mixture with electric mixer, on high speed, about 4 minutes or until mixture is thick and holds its shape.
6 Working quickly, spoon the mixture into pan holes. Sprinkle marshmallow tops with a little of the coconut to cover top evenly. Stand at room temperature about 2 hours or until firm.
7 Place remaining coconut on large tray; gently toss marshmallows to coat in coconut.

preparation time *20 minutes (plus cooling and standing time)*
cooking time *20 minutes* makes *24*
nutritional count per marshmallow *4.4g total fat (3.8g saturated fat); 355kJ (85 cal); 9.8g carbohydrate; 1g protein; 1.4g fibre*

tips Store marshmallows in an airtight container at room temperature for up to two weeks.
You need four passionfruit to get the required amount of pulp.

CHOC-TOFFEE NUTS

¾ cup (110g) slivered almonds
¾ cup (110g) coarsely chopped roasted hazelnuts
¼ cup (55g) caster sugar
1 tablespoon orange juice
2 teaspoons finely grated orange rind
250g dark eating chocolate, melted

1   Preheat oven to 180°C/160°C fan-forced. Line
two 12-hole (1-tablespoon/20ml) mini muffin pans
with paper cases.
2   Combine nuts, sugar and juice in small bowl. Spread
mixture onto greased oven tray. Bake, stirring occasionally,
about 15 minutes or until browned lightly.
3   Remove nut mixture from oven; add rind. Stir to combine
rind and break up nut mixture. Cool.
4   Combine nut mixture with chocolate in medium bowl.
Divide mixture among paper cases. Stand at room
temperature until set.
preparation time *20 minutes*
(plus cooling and standing time)
cooking time *15 minutes* makes *24*
nutritional count per piece *8.4g total fat*
(2.1g saturated fat); 514kJ (123 cal);
9.3g carbohydrate; 2.2g protein; 1g fibre

tip   We used freeform paper cases made by pushing
an 8cm square of baking paper into greased pan holes.

JEWELLED MACAROONS

1 egg white
¼ cup (55g) caster sugar
¾ cup (60g) shredded coconut
2 tablespoons finely chopped glacé apricot
2 tablespoons finely chopped glacé pineapple
2 tablespoons finely chopped glacé red cherries
2 tablespoons finely chopped glacé green cherries
2 tablespoons finely chopped unsalted,
   roasted pistachios

1   Preheat oven to 150°C/130°C fan-forced. Line
two 12-hole (1-tablespoon/20ml) mini muffin pans
with paper cases.
2   Beat egg white in small bowl with electric mixer until
soft peaks form; gradually add sugar, beating until
dissolved between additions. Fold coconut and half the
combined fruit and nuts into egg white mixture.
3   Divide mixture among paper cases. Sprinkle with
remaining fruit and nut mixture. Bake about 20 minutes;
cool macaroons in pans.
preparation time *25 minutes (plus cooling time)*
cooking time *20 minutes* makes *24*
nutritional count per macaroon *2.1g total fat*
(1.5g saturated fat); 201kJ (48 cal);
6.3g carbohydrate; 0.5g protein; 0.5g fibre

tips   Cover macaroons with foil halfway through baking
time if fruit on top starts to brown.
You need approximately 50g of each glacé fruit.

choc-toffee nuts

jewelled macaroons

CHOCOLATE TARTLETS

150g dark eating chocolate
¼ cup (60ml) thickened cream
1 tablespoon orange-flavoured liqueur
1 egg
2 egg yolks
2 tablespoons caster sugar

pastry
1⅔ cups (250g) plain flour
⅓ cup (75g) caster sugar
150g cold butter, chopped coarsely
1 egg yolk

1   Make pastry.
2   Grease two 12-hole (2-tablespoons/40ml) deep flat-based patty pans.
3   Roll pastry between sheets of baking paper to 3mm thickness; cut out twenty-four 6.5cm rounds. Press rounds into pan holes; prick bases all over with fork. Refrigerate 30 minutes.
4   Preheat oven to 200°C/180°C fan-forced.
5   Bake pastry cases 10 minutes. Cool.
6   Reduce temperature to 180°C/160°C fan-forced.
7   Combine chocolate, cream and liqueur in small saucepan; stir over low heat until smooth. Cool 5 minutes.
8   Meanwhile, beat egg, egg yolks and sugar in small bowl with electric mixer until light and fluffy; fold chocolate mixture into egg mixture.
9   Divide filling among pastry cases. Bake 8 minutes; cool 10 minutes. Refrigerate 1 hour. Serve dusted with a little sifted cocoa powder.
pastry Process flour, sugar and butter until coarse. Add egg yolk; process until combined. Knead pastry on floured surface until smooth. Cover; refrigerate 30 minutes.
preparation time *25 minutes (plus refrigeration time)* cooking time *20 minutes* makes *24*
nutritional count per tartlet *8.9g total fat (5.4g saturated fat); 656kJ (157 cal); 16.5g carbohydrate; 2.2g protein; 0.5g fibre*

tip If pastry is too dry, add 2 teaspoons of water with the egg yolk.

MINI TOFFEE APPLES

2 medium red apples (300g)
1 tablespoon lemon juice
3 cups (660g) caster sugar
1 cup (250ml) water

1 Preheat oven to 100°C/80°C fan-forced. Grease two 12-hole (1-tablespoon/20ml) mini muffin pans.
2 Cut unpeeled apples into 0.5cm cubes; combine in small bowl with juice. Spread apple onto baking-paper-lined oven tray. Bake, uncovered, about 40 minutes or until dried.
3 Meanwhile, stir sugar and the water in medium heavy-based saucepan over heat until sugar dissolves. Bring to the boil; boil about 10 minutes, without stirring, or until toffee turns golden brown. Remove pan from heat; allow bubbles to subside.
4 Divide apple among pan holes. Pour toffee slowly over apple; cool toffees about 10 minutes.
5 Cut each paddle pop stick in half. Position half a stick, cut-side down, in centre of each toffee; cool. Using sharp, pointed knife, carefully insert down one side of each pan hole to loosen toffee from edge of pan.
preparation time *25 minutes (plus cooling time)*
cooking time *12 minutes* makes *24*
nutritional count per toffee apple *0g total fat (0g saturated fat); 489kJ (117 cal); 28.8g carbohydrate; 0g protein; 0.2g fibre*

tips Red delicious are the best apples to use. You need 12 paddle pop sticks for this recipe. Gently twist the sticks then pull to remove toffees from pan. Using a saucepan with a pouring lip makes it easy to pour the hot toffee into the pans.

MADELEINES

2 eggs
2 tablespoons caster sugar
2 tablespoons icing sugar
¼ cup (35g) self-raising flour
¼ cup (35g) plain flour
75g unsalted butter, melted
1 tablespoon water
2 tablespoons icing sugar, extra

1 Preheat oven to 200°C/180°C fan-forced. Grease two 12-hole (1½-tablespoons/30ml) madeleine pans.
2 Beat eggs and sifted sugars in small bowl with electric mixer until thick and creamy.
3 Meanwhile, triple-sift flours; sift flour over egg mixture. Pour combined butter and the water down side of bowl then fold ingredients together.
4 Drop rounded tablespoons of mixture into each pan hole. Bake about 10 minutes. Tap hot pan firmly on bench to release madeleines then turn, top-side down, onto wire rack to cool. Serve dusted with sifted extra icing sugar.
preparation time *15 minutes*
cooking time *10 minutes* makes *24*
nutritional count per madeleine *3.1g total fat (1.9g saturated fat); 222kJ (53 cal); 5.4g carbohydrate; 0.9g protein; 0.1g fibre*

variation
orange madeleines Add 1 teaspoon finely grated orange rind when beating the egg mixture. Omit the water and replace with 1 tablespoon orange juice.

mini toffee apples

madeleines

BAKING PANS

Baking pans come in a variety of shapes and sizes, and in an increasing array of finishes including aluminium, tin, silicone and non-stick coating. If your tray is made of tin or has a non-stick coating, you should cook for slightly less time, and drop the oven temperature by about 10°C. When using silicone trays, follow the manufacturer's instructions as there may be cooking time and temperature variations.

We prefer to grease trays coated with a non-stick surface, especially if they are scratched. When greasing pans, you can use either softened butter or cooking-oil spray. We favour butter, particularly in sweet recipes.

1. **shallow round-based patty pan** This pan is only available in a frame of 12 holes of 1½-tablespoons/30ml capacity each. They have a rounded base and are also known as tartlet pans.

2. **deep flat-based patty pan** A flat-based patty pan that usually has 12 round holes with a capacity of 2-tablespoons/40ml each.

3. **muffin pan** Round, flat-based pans with a hole capacity of ⅓-cup/80ml. Commonly available in 12-hole, but also sometimes found in 24-hole size.

4. **texas muffin pan** Texas, or giant, muffins are made in these large, flat-based, round pans that are usually sold as 6-hole pans of ¾-cup/180ml capacity each.

5. **friand pan** These flat-based, oval pans used to be available as individual pans of ½-cup capacity. They are now sold as 6- or 12-hole (½-cup/125ml) pans. If you have individual friand pans, stand them on an oven tray to cook.

6. **mini muffin pan** Mini muffin pans consist of tiny round holes of 1-tablespoon/20ml capacity with a flat base. They are available in a frame of 6, 12 or 24 holes.

7. **petite loaf pan** Petite loaf pans are available in a variety of capacity sizes, ranging from ½ cup to 2 cups. They are all rectangular in shape and quite deep. Petite loaf pans can be sold individually, or in a frame of either 8 or 12 holes. In this book, we have used a 8-hole ½-cup/125ml capacity pan.

8. **madeleine pan** Used solely for making French madeleine cakes, these are available as 12-hole pans of 1½-tablespoons/30ml capacity. Serve cakes top-side down to display the shape of the distinctive shell-like fluting of the moulds.

GLOSSARY

ALMOND a flat, pointy-ended nut with a pitted brown shell and a creamy white kernel that is covered by a brown skin.
meal also known as ground almonds; powdered to a coarse flour-like texture.
slivered small lengthways-cut pieces.

ARBORIO RICE small, round-grain rice, well-suited to absorb a large amount of liquid; especially suitable for risottos.

BAKING PAPER also known as silicon or parchment paper or non-stick baking paper; do not confuse with greaseproof or waxed paper. Used to line pans before cooking or baking; also used to make piping bags.

BICARBONATE OF SODA also known as baking or carb soda; a mild alkali used as a leavening agent in baking.

BISCUITS
Choc Ripple a crunchy chocolate biscuit made with pure cocoa. It was originally developed in the late 1940s as a biscuit that used up left over chocolate-coated biscuits. They quickly became so popular that a special recipe was developed.
Butternut Snap Cookie a crunchy cookie with golden syrup, oats and coconut.

BLOOD ORANGE a virtually seedless citrus fruit with blood-red rind and flesh; it has a sweet, non-acidic pulp and juice with slight strawberry or raspberry overtones. The rind is not as bitter as that of an ordinary orange.

BREADCRUMBS
packaged fine-textured, crunchy, purchased white breadcrumbs.
stale one- or two-day-old bread made into crumbs by grating, blending or processing.

BUTTERMILK originally the term given to the slightly sour liquid left after butter was churned from cream, today it is made similarly to yogurt. Sold alongside all fresh milk products in supermarkets. Despite the implication of its name, it is low in fat.

CAPSICUM also known as bell pepper or, simply, pepper; found in red, green, yellow, orange or purplish-black varieties. Discard seeds and membranes before use.

CARAWAY SEEDS a member of the parsley family having a sharp anise flavour; available in seed or ground form.

CAYENNE PEPPER a thin fleshed, long red, extremely hot, dried, ground chilli.

CHEESE
blue mould-treated cheeses mottled with blue veining. Varieties include firm and crumbly stilton types to mild, creamy brie-like cheeses.

brie often referred to as the "queen of cheeses"; has a bloomy white rind and a creamy centre that becomes runnier as it ripens.
cream also known as Philadelphia or Philly; a soft cows-milk cheese sold at supermarkets in bulk and packaged. Also available as spreadable light cream cheese, which is a blend of cottage and cream cheeses.
goat made from goats milk; has an earthy, strong taste and is available in both soft and firm textures, in various shapes and sizes, and sometimes rolled in ash or herbs.
mascarpone a cultured cream product made in much the same way as yogurt. It's whitish to creamy yellow in colour with a soft, creamy texture and a slightly tangy taste.
parmesan also known as parmigiana; is a hard, grainy, cows-milk cheese. The curd is salted in brine for a month before being aged for up to two years in humid conditions.
pizza a commercial blend of grated mozzarella, cheddar and parmesan.
ricotta the name for this soft, white, cows-milk cheese roughly translates as "cooked again". It's made from whey, a by-product of other cheese-making. Is a sweet, moist cheese with a slightly grainy texture.

CHILLI always use rubber gloves when seeding and chopping fresh chillies as they can burn your skin. We use unseeded chillies in our recipes because the seeds contain the heat; use fewer chillies rather than seeding the lot.
flakes also sold as crushed chilli; dried deep-red, extremely fine slices and seeds.
long red available both fresh and dried; a generic term used for any moderately hot, long (about 6cm-8cm), thin chilli.
powder the Asian variety is the hottest, made from dried ground thai chillies; can be used instead of fresh chillies in the proportion of ½ teaspoon chilli powder to 1 medium chopped fresh red chilli.
thai also known as "scuds"; tiny, very hot and bright red in colour.

CHOCOLATE
Choc Bits also known as chocolate chips or chocolate morsels; available in milk, white and dark chocolate. Good for decorating and hold their shape in baking.
chocolate-hazelnut spread we use Nutella. It was originally developed when chocolate was hard to source during World War 2; hazelnuts were added to extend the chocolate supply.

dark eating also known as semi-sweet or luxury chocolate; made of a high percentage of cocoa liquor and cocoa butter, and a little added sugar.
milk eating very popular eating chocolate, mild and very sweet; similar in make-up to dark chocolate with the difference being the addition of milk solids.
white eating contains no cocoa solids but derives its sweet flavour from cocoa butter. Very sensitive to heat.

CHORIZO sausage of Spanish origin; made of coarsely ground pork and highly seasoned with garlic and chilli.

COCONUT
cream obtained commercially from the first pressing of the coconut flesh alone, without the addition of water. Available in cans and cartons at most supermarkets.
desiccated concentrated, unsweetened, dried and finely shredded coconut flesh.
milk not the liquid found inside the fruit, which is called coconut water, but the diluted liquid from the second pressing of the white flesh of a mature coconut.
shredded unsweetened thin strips of dried coconut flesh.

CORIANDER also known as pak chee, cilantro or chinese parsley; bright-green leafy herb with a pungent flavour. Both the stems and roots of coriander are also used in Thai cooking; wash well before using. Coriander seeds are also available but are no substitute for fresh coriander, as the taste is very different.

CREAM we use fresh cream, also known as pure cream and pouring cream, unless otherwise stated.
thickened a whipping cream containing a thickener.

CROISSANT the French word for crescent. A rich, flaky pastry breakfast roll shaped as a crescent with a crisp texture on the outside, and a flaky layered soft buttery centre.

CUCUMBER, LEBANESE short, slender and thin-skinned. Probably the most popular variety because of its tender, edible skin, tiny, yielding seeds and sweet, fresh, flavoursome taste.

CUSTARD POWDER instant mixture used to make pouring custard; similar to North American instant pudding mixes.

DRIED CRANBERRIES have the same slightly sour, succulent flavour as fresh cranberries. Can usually be substituted for or with other dried fruit in most recipes. Available in most supermarkets. Also available in a sweetened form.

EGGPLANT also known as aubergine; actually a fruit and belongs to the same family as the tomato, chilli and potato. Ranges in size from tiny to very large and in colour from pale green to deep purple.
baby also known as finger or japanese eggplant; very small and slender so can be used without disgorging (salting).

FENNEL also known as finocchio or anise; a roundish, crunchy, pale green-white vegetable. The bulb has a slightly sweet, anise flavour but the leaves have a much stronger taste. Also sometimes the name given to the dried seeds of the plant, which have a stronger licorice flavour.

FISH
firm white fish fillet blue eye, bream, swordfish, ling, whiting or sea perch are all good choices. Check for any small pieces of bone in the fillets and use tweezers to remove them.
ocean trout a farmed fish with pink, soft flesh. It is from the same family as the atlantic salmon; one can be substituted for the other. Also available smoked.

FLOUR
cornflour also known as cornstarch. Available made from corn or wheat; used as a thickening agent in cooking.
plain an all-purpose wheat flour.
self-raising plain flour sifted with baking powder in the proportion of 1 cup flour to 2 teaspoons baking powder.
wholemeal self-raising flour milled from the whole wheat grain to which leavening agents have been added.

FRIED SHALLOT (homm jiew) served as a condiment on Asian tables to be sprinkled over just-cooked food. Found in cellophane bags or jars at all Asian grocery shops; once opened, they will keep for months if stored tightly sealed. Make your own by frying thinly sliced peeled shallots until golden and crisp.

GARLIC CHIVES have rougher, flatter leaves than simple chives, and possess a pink-tinged teardrop-shaped flowering bud at the end; used as a salad green, or steamed and eaten as a vegetable.

GELATINE a thickening agent. Available in sheet form, known as leaf gelatine, or as a powder. Three teaspoons of dried gelatine (8g or one sachet) is roughly equivalent to four gelatine leaves.

GINGER, FRESH also known as green or root ginger; the thick gnarled root of a tropical plant.

GLACÉ FRUIT any fruit that has been preserved in a sugar syrup.

KAFFIR LIME LEAVES also known as bai magrood. Look like two glossy dark green leaves joined end to end, forming a rounded hourglass shape. Sold fresh, dried or frozen, the dried leaves are less potent so double the number if using them as a substitute for fresh. A strip of fresh lime peel may be substituted for each kaffir lime leaf.

LEMON GRASS a tall, clumping, lemon-smelling and -tasting, sharp-edged grass; the white lower part of each stem is chopped and used in Asian cooking.

LEMON THYME a member of the mint family with tiny grey-green leaves. The lemon scent is due to the high level of citral in its leaves – an oil also found in lemon, orange, verbena and lemon grass. The citrus scent is enhanced by crushing the leaves in your hands before using the herb.

LIQUEUR
coffee-flavoured we use either Kahlua or Tia Maria coffee-flavoured liqueurs.
orange-flavoured we use either Grand Marnier (an orange-flavoured liqueur) or Cointreau (a citrus-flavoured liqueur).

NESTLÉ TOP 'N' FILL CARAMEL a delicious filling made from milk and cane sugar. Has similar qualities to sweetened condensed milk, only a thicker, caramel consistency, which is great to use in caramel desserts.

OIL
cooking spray we use a cholesterol-free cooking spray made from canola oil.
olive made from ripened olives. Extra virgin and virgin are the best, while extra light or light refers to taste not fat levels.
peanut pressed from ground peanuts; most commonly used oil in Asian cooking because of its high smoke point (capacity to handle high heat without burning).
sesame made from roasted, crushed, white sesame seeds; a flavouring rather than a cooking medium.
vegetable sourced from plants.

ONION
brown and white are interchangeable. Their pungent flesh adds flavour to a vast range of dishes.
green also known as scallion or, incorrectly, shallot; an immature onion picked before the bulb has formed, having a long, bright-green edible stalk.
spring onions with small white bulbs and long green leaves with narrow tops.
red also known as spanish, red spanish or bermuda onion; a sweet-flavoured, large, purple-red onion.

ORANGE BLOSSOM WATER also known as orange flower water; a concentrated flavouring made from orange blossoms. Available from Middle-Eastern food stores and some supermarkets and delicatessens. Cannot be substituted with citrus flavourings, as the taste is completely different.

PANCETTA Italian bacon that is cured but not smoked.

PAPAYA also known as pawpaw or papaw; a large, pear-shaped red-orange tropical fruit. Sometimes used unripe (green) in cooking.

PASTRY, READY-ROLLED packaged sheets of frozen pastry, available from most supermarkets.
fillo is unique in that no margarine or fat is added to the dough. The dough is very elastic in texture and not rolled like other pastries, but stretched to the desired thickness. This gives it its unique, delicate, tissue thin sheets. It is best brushed with margarine or butter before baking.
puff a crisp, light pastry; layers of dough and margarine are folded and rolled many times making many layers. When baked, it becomes a high, crisp, flaky pastry. Butter puff pastry uses butter for the shortening, whereas puff pastry uses a commercially made blend of vegetable and animal fats.
shortcrust is a tender, crunchy, melt in the mouth buttery pastry. Once baked it is a light, crumbly easily broken pastry.

PEPITAS pale green kernels of dried pumpkin seeds; available plain or salted.

PINE NUT also known as pignoli; not in fact a nut but a small, cream-coloured kernel from pine cones.

POLENTA also known as cornmeal. A flour-like cereal made of dried corn (maize); sold ground in several different textures. Also the name of the dish made from it.

POMEGRANATE a round juicy fruit the size of a large orange, with leathery red skin. Contains white seeds in a pinkish-red flesh, which can be purchased dried and ground; they add an acidic piquancy to vegetarian dishes.

POPPY SEEDS small, dried, bluish-grey seeds of the poppy plant. Poppy seeds have a crunchy texture and a nutty flavour. They can be purchased whole or ground in most supermarkets. Because of their high oil content, they are prone to rancidity and should be stored, refrigerated, in an airtight container for up to six months.

PRESERVED LEMON a North African speciality, the citrus is preserved, usually whole, in a mixture of salt and lemon juice. To use, remove and discard pulp, squeeze juice from rind, rinse rind well then slice. Sold in jars or in bulk by delicatessens; once opened, store preserved lemon in the refrigerator.

PROSCIUTTO cured, air-dried, unsmoked, pressed ham.

ROCKET LEAVES also known as rucola, arugula and rugula; a peppery-tasting green leaf that can be used similarly to baby spinach leaves, eaten raw in salads or used in cooking. Baby rocket leaves are both smaller and less peppery.

SAFFRON THREADS available in strands or ground form; imparts a yellow-orange colour to food once infused. Quality varies greatly; the best is the most expensive spice in the world. Should be stored in the freezer.

SAUCES

barbecue a spicy, tomato-based sauce used to marinate or as a condiment.

chilli we use a hot Chinese variety made from red thai chillies, salt and vinegar. Use sparingly, increasing the quantity to suit your taste.

cranberry made of cranberries cooked in sugar syrup; has an astringent flavour.

fish also called nam pla or nuoc nam; made from pulverised salted fermented fish, most often anchovies. Has a pungent smell and strong taste; use sparingly.

hoisin a thick, sweet and spicy Chinese paste made from salted fermented soya beans, onions and garlic; used as a marinade or baste.

oyster Asian in origin, this rich, brown sauce is made from oysters and their brine, cooked with salt and soy sauce, and thickened with starches.

soy made from fermented soya beans. Several variations are available in most supermarkets and Asian food stores. *Dark soy* is deep brown, almost black in colour; rich, with a thicker consistency than other types. Pungent, but not particularly salty; is good for marinating. *Japanese soy* is an all-purpose low-sodium sauce made with more wheat content than its Chinese counterparts. Possibly the best table soy and the one to choose if you only want one variety. *Light soy* is a fairly thin, pale and salty tasting sauce; used in dishes in which the natural colour of the ingredients is to be maintained. Not to be confused with salt-reduced or low-sodium soy sauces.

sweet chilli a thin, mild sauce made from red chillies, sugar, garlic and vinegar.

tomato also known as ketchup or catsup; made from tomatoes, vinegar and spices.

worcestershire a dark-coloured condiment made from garlic, soy sauce, tamarind, lime, onions, molasses, anchovies, vinegar and seasonings.

SESAME SEEDS black and white are the most common of this small oval seed, however, there are also red and brown varieties. To toast, spread the seeds in a heavy-based frying pan; toast briefly over low heat.

SHALLOTS also called french shallots, golden shallots or eschalots. Small, elongated, brown-skinned members of the onion family.

SILVER BEET also known as swiss chard and, incorrectly, spinach; has fleshy stalks and large dark-green leaves.

SNICKERS BAR a confection made of peanut butter nougat topped with roasted peanuts and caramel, and covered with milk chocolate.

SPINACH also known as english spinach and, incorrectly, silver beet.

STOCK available in cans, bottles or tetra packs. Stock cubes or powder can be used. As a guide, 1 teaspoon of stock powder or 1 small crumbled stock cube mixed with 1 cup (250ml) water will give a fairly strong stock. Be aware of the salt and fat content of stock cubes and powders and prepared stocks.

SUGAR

brown a soft, finely granulated sugar retaining molasses for its characteristic colour and flavour.

caster also known as superfine or finely granulated table sugar.

demerara small-grained golden-coloured crystal sugar.

icing sugar also known as confectioners' sugar or powdered sugar; granulated sugar crushed with a small amount of cornflour added.

white a coarse, granulated table sugar, also known as crystal sugar.

SUMAC a purple-red, astringent spice with a tart, lemony flavour. Ground from berries growing on shrubs that flourish wild around the Mediterranean.

SWEET SHERRY fortified wine used in cooking or consumed as an aperitif. Sherries differ in colour and flavour; sold as fino (light, dry), amontillado (medium sweet, dark) and oloroso (full-bodied, very dark).

SWEETENED CONDENSED MILK a canned milk product consisting of milk with more than half the water content removed and sugar added to the remaining milk.

SYRUPS

glucose also known as liquid glucose; made from wheat starch and used in jam and confectionery making. Available at health-food stores and supermarkets.

golden a thick, golden-coloured by-product of refined sugar cane; pure maple syrup or honey can be substituted.

maple distilled from the sap of maple trees. Maple-flavoured syrup or pancake syrup is not an adequate substitute for the real thing.

TACO SEASONING MIX a packaged seasoning meant to duplicate the mexican sauce made from oregano, cumin, chillies and other spices. Found in supermarkets.

TIKKA MASALA PASTE in Indian cooking the word "masala" loosely translates as paste and the word "tikka" means a bite-sized piece of meat, poultry or fish. Usually consists of chilli, coriander, cumin, lentil flour, garlic, ginger, oil, turmeric, fennel, pepper, cloves, cinnamon and cardamom.

TOFU also known as soya bean curd or bean curd.

VANILLA

bean dried, long, thin pod from a tropical golden orchid grown in central and South America and Tahiti; the tiny black seeds inside the bean impart a luscious vanilla flavour. Place a whole bean in a jar of sugar to make the vanilla sugar often called for in recipes; a bean can be used three or four times before losing its flavour.

extract obtained from vanilla beans infused in water.

VINEGAR

red wine made from red wine.

white wine made from white wine.

WOMBOK also known as peking cabbage, chinese cabbage or petsai. Elongated in shape with pale green, crinkly leaves; this is the most common cabbage in South-East Asian cooking. Can be shredded or chopped and eaten raw, braised, steamed or stir-fried.

ZUCCHINI also known as courgette; a small pale- or dark-green, yellow or white vegetable belonging to the squash family. Harvested when young, its edible flowers can be stuffed then deep-fried or oven-baked to make a delicious appetiser.

CONVERSION CHART

MEASURES

One Australian metric measuring cup holds approximately 250ml; one Australian metric tablespoon holds 20ml; one Australian metric teaspoon holds 5ml.

The difference between one country's measuring cups and another's is within a two- or three-teaspoon variance, and will not affect your cooking results. North America, New Zealand and the United Kingdom use a 15ml tablespoon.

All cup and spoon measurements are level. The most accurate way of measuring dry ingredients is to weigh them. When measuring liquids,
use a clear glass or plastic jug with the metric markings.

We use large eggs with an average weight of 60g.

DRY MEASURES

METRIC	IMPERIAL
15g	½oz
30g	1oz
60g	2oz
90g	3oz
125g	4oz (¼lb)
155g	5oz
185g	6oz
220g	7oz
250g	8oz (½lb)
280g	9oz
315g	10oz
345g	11oz
375g	12oz (¾lb)
410g	13oz
440g	14oz
470g	15oz
500g	16oz (1lb)
750g	24oz (1½lb)
1kg	32oz (2lb)

LIQUID MEASURES

METRIC	IMPERIAL
30ml	1 fluid oz
60ml	2 fluid oz
100ml	3 fluid oz
125ml	4 fluid oz
150ml	5 fluid oz (¼ pint/1 gill)
190ml	6 fluid oz
250ml	8 fluid oz
300ml	10 fluid oz (½ pint)
500ml	16 fluid oz
600ml	20 fluid oz (1 pint)
1000ml (1 litre)	1¾ pints

LENGTH MEASURES

METRIC	IMPERIAL
3mm	⅛ in
6mm	¼in
1cm	½in
2cm	¾in
2.5cm	1in
5cm	2in
6cm	2½in
8cm	3in
10cm	4in
13cm	5in
15cm	6in
18cm	7in
20cm	8in
23cm	9in
25cm	10in
28cm	11in
30cm	12in (1ft)

OVEN TEMPERATURES

These oven temperatures are only a guide for conventional ovens. For fan-forced ovens, check the manufacturer's manual.

	°C (CELSIUS)	°F (FAHRENHEIT)	GAS MARK
Very slow	120	250	½
Slow	150	275-300	1-2
Moderately slow	160	325	3
Moderate	180	350-375	4-5
Moderately hot	200	400	6
Hot	220	425-450	7-8
Very hot	240	475	9

INDEX

If you like this cookbook, you'll love these...

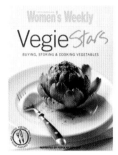

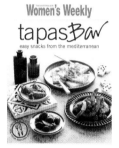

These are just a small selection of titles available in
The Australian Women's Weekly range on sale at selected
newsagents, supermarkets or online at www.acpbooks.com.au

also available in bookstores...

ACP BOOKS

General manager Christine Whiston
Editor-in-chief Susan Tomnay
Creative director & designer Hieu Chi Nguyen
Art director Hannah Blackmore
Senior editor Wendy Bryant
Food director Pamela Clark
Recipe development Cathie Lonnie
Nutritional information Belinda Farlow
Sales & rights director Brian Cearnes
Marketing manager Bridget Cody
Senior business analyst Rebecca Varela
Circulation manager Jama Mclean
Operations manager David Scotto
Production manager Victoria Jefferys

ACP Books are published by ACP Magazines a division of
PBL Media Pty Limited
PBL Media, Chief Executive Officer Ian Law
Publishing & sales director, Women's lifestyle Lynette Phillips
General manager, Editorial projects,
   Women's lifestyle Deborah Thomas
Editor at Large, Women's lifestyle Pat Ingram
Marketing director, Women's lifestyle Matthew Dominello
Commercial manager, Women's lifestyle Seymour Cohen
Research director, Women's lifestyle Justin Stone

Produced by ACP Books, Sydney.

Published by ACP Books, a division of ACP Magazines Ltd,
54 Park St, Sydney; GPO Box 4088, Sydney, NSW 2001.
phone (02) 9282 8618; fax (02) 9267 9438.
acpbooks@acpmagazines.com.au; www.acpbooks.com.au

Printed by Toppan Printing Co, China.

Australia Distributed by Network Services,
phone +61 2 9282 8777; fax +61 2 9264 3278;
networkweb@networkservicescompany.com.au
United Kingdom Distributed by Australian Consolidated Press (UK),
phone (01604) 642 200; fax (01604) 642 300; books@acpuk.com
New Zealand Distributed by Netlink Distribution Company,
phone (9) 366 9966; ask@ndc.co.nz
South Africa Distributed by PSD Promotions,
phone (27 11) 392 6065/6/7; fax (27 11) 392 6079/80;
orders@psdprom.co.za
Canada Distributed by Publishers Group Canada
phone (800) 663 5714; fax (800) 565 3770; service@raincoast.com

Title: Little pies & cakes : the Australian Women's Weekly /
food director, Pamela Clark.
Publisher: Sydney : ACP Books, 2008.
ISBN: 978-1-86396-746-4 (pbk)
Notes: Includes index
Subjects: Cookery. Appetizers. Snack foods.
Other Authors/Contributors: Clark, Pamela
Also Titled: Australian women's weekly.
Dewey Number: 641.821

© ACP Magazines Ltd 2008
ABN 18 053 273 546
This publication is copyright. No part of it may be reproduced or
transmitted in any form without the written permission of the publishers.
First published 2008. Reprinted 2009.

Scanpan cookware is used in the AWW Test Kitchen.

Photographer Gorta Yuuki **Stylist** Margot Braddon
Food preparation Nicole Jennings
Cover Portuguese custard tarts, page 101

To order books, phone 136 116 (within Australia)
or order online at www.acpbooks.com.au
Send recipe enquiries to:
recipeenquiries@acpmagazines.com.au

books